5 THINGS YOU NEVER KNEW ABOUT MARY

Gospels, Apostles, Believers, Reformers, Us

R. A. Varghese

TABLE OF CONTENTS

      How

          1 No Authoritative Interpretation
          2 One Authoritative Interpretation

      What

          Her Words
          Words About Her

              "Kecharitomene" – "Our tainted nature's solitary boast"

              "The Mother of My Lord"

              "A Woman Clothed with the Sun"

          Her Acts

New Eve, Queen-Mother, Mother of Emmanuel, All-Holy Ark of the Covenant, Intercessory Mother of the Faithful, Virgin Mary

Theotokos (Mother of God), Panagia (All-Holy), Heavenly Intercessor, Aeiparthenos (Ever-Virgin)

      <u>Appendices</u>

      Mother of God?

      All-Holy?

      Assumed into Heaven?

      Do Those Who Seek Her Intercession Worship Mary?

      Perpetual Virginity?

All-Holy Virgin Mary, Mother of God, Mother of Believers

A Return to Roots
      Freedom and Salvation
      Mediation
      Intercession

A THANK YOU CARD

Salvation or damnation, Heaven or Hell, the will of God or my own will? Yes or No? This was the choice offered at the inception of humankind. Sadly, the reply was "No" and the consequence a tragedy without end. But then the human race was given a second chance. A young virgin was asked to bear the Messiah of Israel, the Son of the Most High, the Savior. She said "Yes": "May it be done to me according to your word." The result was redemption: the gate of Heaven being opened again through the life, death and resurrection of God incarnate: salvation made possible for all who accept the divine invitation.

So, at the outset, let us say this: Thank you "favored one," thank you Mary, blessed and virginal, for saying "Yes." Thank you for sticking with your "Yes." Thank you for silently bearing the prophesied suffering of the sword through your being. Thank you for remembering and reflecting on it all in your heart. Thank you for saving the day in Cana. Thank you for being the mother of "those who keep God's commandments and bear witness to Jesus."

Let us be mindful here that there is one thing, above all, that matters, one indisputable fact that alone is relevant: Mary of Israel's response to the angelic invitation to be the Mother of the Redeemer meant the difference between damnation and the possibility of salvation for humanity. Fortunately for us all, she said "Yes."

Of course, some speak of her as a mindless instrument of a puppet-master deity who was pre-programmed to say "Yes." But the deity they speak of is not the God revealed in the Bible. In actuality, these fantasists simply evade what is obvious in the Gospels and in our own experience. They live in their own parallel universe.

Mary could easily have said "No" as so many did throughout the biblical narratives. The Old and New Testament texts are essentially accounts of choices and consequences. There was no pre-programming at any point: simply a trail of tears from the beginning, broken by occasional triumphs, featuring unlikely heroes and heroines (Moses the stammerer, David the shepherd boy who would be king, Esther the young protectress of her people, Paul the killer of Christians who became an apostle). In short, life as we know it here and now.

It is precisely because Mary's choice was a fruit of her own free will that her cousin exclaimed: "Blessed are you who believed that what was spoken to you by the Lord would be fulfilled." You are blessed because you believed!

So why is it so hard to accept the obvious, to give credit where it is due, to say "thank you" for saying "Yes?"

But once we get past our self-imposed stumbling blocks, we will discover deeper truths about this "one thing" about Mary. Her "Yes" is ultimately a victory for God. The last word in the human experiment does not go to the Devil and the errant first couple. This would have been the case if redemption was entirely and exclusively a product of divine action. But it was a human person who pulled the trigger that enabled divine intervention, beginning with the conception and birth of the divine-human Savior and culminating in his salvific death and resurrection.

She may be the solitary boast of our "tainted nature" – but she was our boast. And this means that God's "idea" of creating free human persons could not be derailed even by the concerted effort of all the forces of evil. There was at least one human person – the Mother of Jesus – who freely chose the divine plan (Jesus, we remember, was a human being but a divine Person). We see a foreshadowing of this in the case of Job, an instance of God explicitly allowing his followers to be tested by the Evil One. Their victory is his victory.

Mary's "Yes" is thus a divine triumph in the human realm just as the Archangel Michael's "Yes" to God was a divine victory in the angelic domain.

Secondly, the incarnation of God in Christ took place in and through a family: he was the virginal child of a married couple. The participation of the family went beyond the Incarnation and extended to the Son's redemptive mission. In the case of Mary, she was told she would be pierced with a sword as she participated in her Son's mission.

The redemption of humanity was achieved not as a solitary act but an act begotten in solidarity because it was an act into which the Redeemer drew his family. The father and the mother played a supporting role in the lifework of the Son of God made man, in a manner that was irreducibly distinct from the part played by his Apostles and other followers.

They – his family – belonged to an "order" of action in salvation history that radically transcended the role played by all other human persons – they were participants in the mission of Jesus even before his birth! As the leaders of the apostolic community recognized from the very beginning, Mary was the New Eve just as Jesus was the New Adam.

At the center of Incarnation, Redemption and Mediation is the incarnate Word of God who is Redeemer and infinite Mediator. But united with him, GIVEN by him and working with him in a unique and irrevocable mode is his mother, the New Eve and the Mother of all Christians.

Finally, we need to recognize the foundational importance of Mary's "Yes" for our own sakes. The gate of Heaven is open. But there is no guarantee of entry. No matter what some theologies say, the teaching of Jesus in the Gospels is unequivocal: we have to say "Yes" to him and "Yes" on a continuous basis (just read the Gospels). In grasping the "one thing" that is pivotal about Mary, we come to see the urgency of saying "Yes" to God ourselves.

But this meditation on Mary and her "Yes" is not intended simply as an academic exercise. It is meant to show that the Mother of Jesus is our Mother who helps us with our own continuing "Yes" to God.

In the din of debate, in the midst of polemics and platitudes, let us not lose sight of this. We are talking about a real, live, always-accessible mother. She was the mother of Jesus. She was named the mother of her Son's beloved disciple. She was finally revealed as the mother of all the faithful. And she was seen as Mother by Christians from the earliest days of Christendom. "We fly to thy patronage, O holy Mother of God" said a prayer from 250 A.D. "Mary is the Mother of Jesus and the mother of us all. If Christ is ours, we must be where he is; and all that he has must be ours, and his mother is therefore also ours," said Martin Luther.

The sooner we turn to her, the sooner she can teach us to do the one thing that is most important in our lives: to say "Yes" to our Savior.

x

TABLE TALK – A SUMMARY OF THE BOOK

Mary – What the Bible Says

All-Holy	The angel Gabriel greets her with the title *Kecharitomene* which is translated as "completely, perfectly, enduringly endowed with grace." (*A Greek Grammar of the New Testament*)
Mother of God	Elizabeth tells Mary, *"How does this happen to me, that the mother of my Lord should come to me?" (Luke 1:43)*. "Lord" here quite clearly refers to "God" because all the other usages of "Lord" in this first chapter of the Gospel of *Luke* concerns Yahweh (God). In *Matthew*, the prophecy in Isaiah is applied to Mary: *"'Behold, the virgin shall be with child and bear a son, and they shall name him Emmanuel,' which means 'God is with us.'" (Matthew 1:23)*. Here she is explicitly called the Mother of God-with-us.
Intercessor	*"When the wine ran short, the mother of Jesus said to him, "They have no wine.' [And] Jesus said to her, 'Woman, how does your concern affect me? My hour has not yet come.' His mother said to the servers, 'Do whatever he tells you.'" (John 2:3-5).* Mary interceded with Jesus on behalf of the wedding host and he grants her request although it was not part of the divine timetable. Mary non-verbally knew that Jesus was going to grant her request because she tells the servants to prepare for his instructions. When Jesus says, "My hour has not yet come," he is informing her that he will respond to her intercession when his "hour", the hour of glorification, comes. From Jesus' own words, we see that he is telling his Mother to intercede with him once he has been glorified and is with the Father.
Assumed into Heaven	*"A great sign appeared in the sky, a woman clothed with the sun, with the moon under her feet, and on her head a crown of twelve stars. She was with child … She gave birth to a son, a male child, destined to rule all the nations with an iron rod." (Revelation 12:1,5)* The "woman clothed with the sun," given the language used, is from Heaven. The Son born to her is Jesus the Messiah which means she is Mary.
Mother of All Christians	*"Then the dragon became angry with the woman and went off to wage war against the rest of her offspring, those who keep God's commandments and bear witness to Jesus." (Revelation 12:17).* The Mother of Jesus, Mary, is also the mother of who all bear witness to him and keep the commandments of God.
To be venerated	*"When Elizabeth heard Mary's greeting, the infant leaped in her womb, and Elizabeth, filled with the holy Spirit, cried out in a loud voice and said, "Most blessed are you among women, and blessed is the fruit of your womb. And how does this happen to me, that the mother of my Lord should come to me? For at the moment the sound of your greeting reached my ears, the infant in my womb leaped for joy. Blessed are you who believed that what was spoken to you by the Lord would be fulfilled." And Mary said: … behold, from now on will all ages call me blessed." (Luke 1:41-46,48).* Scripture says that Mary is to be "blessed" because she "believed" and that "all ages" are to call her "blessed." It was at the sound of *her* voice that "the infant … leaped for joy."

How can we KNOW what the Bible Means? – Two Approaches

Approach	Result
#1 No Authoritative Interpretation Develop and follow your individual interpretation and/or follow the interpretation developed by preachers or theologians of the second millennium of Christianity and later	Different Christian groups (all claiming to be led by the Holy Spirit) have different, even contradictory, views on fundamental theological matters: the identity of Jesus; the inner being of God; salvation; mediation; the working of the Holy Spirit. No certainty on which interpretation is authentic. Non-Trinitarian groups have sprouted even from staunch Bible-believing denominations (e.g., Oneness Pentecostals). Varying beliefs on what is meant by of the divine inspiration of the Old and New Testaments including denial of their divine inspiration.
#2 One Authoritative Interpretation Accept and proclaim the interpretation of the apostolic community, which also determined and fixed the canon of the New Testament, and the believers of the first millennium of Christianity.	Organic unity of doctrine on the incarnation of God in Jesus; the Trinity; Mary, the Mother of Jesus; salvation as a gift of grace that can be accepted or rejected; mediation by believers on behalf of each other. This body of teaching has been proclaimed and propagated for twenty centuries despite numerous influential and conflicting world-views that have come and gone. Proclamation of the Old and New Testaments as the inspired Word of God.

The conclusion is clear: either the interpretation of biblical texts made by the apostolic community has to be taken as authoritative and, hence, the only authentic interpretation *OR we cannot even accept the New Testament as Scripture since it is this apostolic community that made the "interpretation" as to which books are divinely inspired and worthy of inclusion in the canon of Scripture.*

Mary – What the New Testament Apostolic Community Proclaimed

Role	Fathers	Liturgies	Devotions
New Eve	✓	✓	✓
Queen Mother	✓	✓	✓
Mother of Emmanuel	✓	✓	✓
All-Holy Ark of the Covenant	✓	✓	✓
Intercessory Mother of the Faithful	✓	✓	✓
Virgin	✓	✓	✓

Mary – What All First Millennium Christians Affirmed

Role	Council	Liturgies
Theotokos (Mother of God)	✓	✓
Panagia (All-Holy)	✓	✓
Heavenly Intercessor	✓	✓
Aeiparthenos (Ever-Virgin)	✓	✓

What the Protestant Reformers and Modern Protestant Thinkers Professed

Teaching About Mary	Luther	Calvin	Zwingli
Mother of God	✓	✓	✓
All-Holy	✓		✓
Virgin	✓	✓	✓
Assumed into Heaven	✓		✓
To be honored	✓	✓	✓

Mary – What the New Testament Apostolic Community Proclaimed

Action	Bible	Faathers	Councils	Liturgies
Honor	✓	✓	✓	✓
Venerate	✓	✓	✓	✓
Enter into filial relationship	✓	✓	✓	✓
Seek intercession	✓	✓	✓	✓

INTRODUCTION

The odyssey of the Blessed Virgin Mary is one of the most astonishing tales in the history of humanity. But it is so familiar we take it for granted. And so we fail to realize its utterly remarkable nature.

Here was a human person whose Son was God incarnate – and whose mother she remains for all eternity. A person who entered into the most intimate union possible union for a human person with God the Holy Spirit. A person specially chosen and prepared by God the Father to be not just the Mother of his only begotten Son (*Luke* 1:30) but of all who bear witness to the Son and keep the divine commandments (*Revelation* 12:17).

Most important, the Incarnation of God the Son was contingent on her consent – a consent she granted from the depths of her being. She was called to share totally in the sorrow that was to be his life (*Luke* 2:30) – a participation she whole-heartedly offered up. The earliest apprehension of her by the faithful was, in fact, in her role as Sorrowful Mother.

Our salvation comes from Christ Jesus. But the salvific coming of Christ was made possible by his Mother's free act of obedience to the divine Will. She was not a puppet, not a mindless vessel chosen by a super-human puppet-master to achieve his aims as some critics of Marian devotion have said. Such critics are ideologists who deny the plain words of Scripture and devalue both the dignity of the human person and the gift of freewill given by our Maker.

Scripture tell us that she was not simply chosen by God but that Mary herself chose God in the most important choice ever made by a human person. Therein lies her blessedness through all generations. "Blessed are *you who believed* that what was spoken to you by the Lord would be fulfilled." (*Luke* 1:45). As memories fade and attention-spans diminish, we have to constantly remind ourselves of the magnitude of this act. As Baptist minister and scholar Willie James Jennings pithily put it, "Salvation begins with Mary's yes."[1]

Lutheran theologian David Yeago sees her "Yes" as a continuous process:

> Even after the birth of Jesus … in the story of his presentation in Temple, Mary is mysteriously acknowledged in the Lukan account as having a *continuing* role in the story of salvation. … As the one addressed in this singular way by the election and promise of God, Mary is not simply a private person but a *public* one; she is called by the angel's proclamation to an *office*, a public role within the communion of God's people and the history of God's salvation. …

> Mary stands at the intersection of the Old Covenant and the New. In her, by God's election and grace, the drama of Old Covenant Israel reaches its turning point, and the vocation of renewed Israel, the Messianic assembly, the Christian church, is prototypically embodied. She is 'Daughter Zion' (Zeph 3:14; Zech 9:9). …

> Precisely as one who *persists* in her consent to God's proclamation and promise through the course of a temporal

pilgrimage, she is also the archbeliever and the archprophet of the New Covenant, the one who paradigmatically receives the reign of God by faith and renders it present in power to the world, all the while walking 'in the dim light of faith.' She thus articulates in her own being the constant *form* of the existence of the people of God at *every* point in the story of salvation."[2]

So, what role does the Mother of Jesus, play in the rest of the Christian story and in our journey to God?

From the very beginning, the Christian community recognized her pivotal role in the divine scheme of salvation. We see this in the biblical texts, the prayers of the earliest Christian communities, the writings of the first Christian thought-leaders, the doctrines of the undivided Church and the unchanging devotions of Christendom.

Today, however, some Christians hold that Marian doctrines and devotions are unbiblical, superstitious and idolatrous. Such anti-Marian ideas did not originate in the Reformation since (as we shall see) its architects held to most of the classical teachings on Mary. Rather, as Lutheran scholars like Frederick Heiler and Basilea Schlink have shown, their origin can be traced to the Enlightenment and Rationalism.

Heiler attributes the deviation to "the spirit of the Enlightenment with its lack of understanding of mystery, and especially of the mystery of the Incarnation, which in the 18th century began the work of destruction."[3]

Schlink writes that "the majority of us have drifted away from the proper attitude towards her ... which Martin Luther had indicated to us on the basis of Holy Scripture .... All biblical relationship to the Mother Mary was lost, and we are still suffering from this heritage."[4]

Sadly, as pointed out by Anglican scholar Allan Lancashire, this abandonment of Mary also led to rejection of her Son: "A rejection of Mariology must inevitably lead to a rejection of orthodox Christology. ... Devotion to Mary, far from leading men away from Christ, draws the Church into a deeper recognition of the mystery of God's loving activity directed towards man in Christ."[5]

As we will be seeing, prominent Protestant thinkers – Presbyterians, Baptists, Anglicans/ Episcopalians, Methodists, Lutherans, Evangelicals – have re-discovered the biblical Mary. One of the most insightful books on the Rosary was written by a Methodist. Mary's Immaculate Conception and Assumptiony have been presented in a compelling new light by a renowned Presbyterian theologian. Especially profound and powerful is the contribution of Lutheran thinker Ronald Jenson. In a majestic paean of praise, he proclaims:

> Mary is Israel in one person, as Temple and archprophet and guardian of Torah. To ask her to pray for me is to invoke all God's history with Israel at once, all his place-taking in this people, and all the faithfulness of God to this people, as grounds for his faithfulness to me. It is to have Moses say, 'Why should the heathen profane your name, because you leave your people in the lurch? ...' It is to send Aaron to the Tent of Meeting on my behalf. It is to quote all Scripture's promises about prayer at once, as summed up by Jesus, 'Whatever you ask the Father in my name will be done.'

> '*Fiat mihi*,' Mary said, giving her womb as space for God in this world. After all the Lord's struggle with his beloved Israel, he finally found a place in Israel that unbelief would

not destroy like the Temple, or silence like the prophets, or simply lose, like the Book of the Law before Josiah. This place is a person. To ask Mary to pray for us is to meet him there. [6]

In our inquiry, we consider what Christians affirm about Mary, the Mother of Jesus, and why. Among other things, we will address the concerns and criticisms of the anti-Marian Christians by drawing attention to five sets of facts relating to the role of Mary:

The teaching of the Bible

The faith of the first Christians

The proclamation of the Christian community

The witness of the Protestant Reformers and modern Protestant commentators

The Mother of Jesus seen as the Mother of all Christians as taught by Scripture and recognized as such throughout Christian history

Collectively, as we will see, these five data-sets testify to the truth of the historic Christian consensus on the Mother of Jesus.

6

#1 WHAT THE BIBLE SAYS

Approach to Interpreting the Bible	Characteristics	Results
#1 No Authoritative Interpretation Develop and follow your individual interpretation and/or follow the interpretation developed by preachers or theologians of the second millennium of Christianity and later	Touchstones of truth in interpreting Scripture: • Personal beliefs and opinions • Beliefs propagated by individual preachers, leaders or theologians • Beliefs that are dominant in an era or society Conviction of enlightenment by the Holy Spirit on specific matters (different believers who each claim to be led by the Holy Spirit sometimes come to different conclusions on the same matters)	The emergence of 45,000 denominations (source: Center for Global Christianity) with new ones forming daily. These denominations have different views on fundamental theological matters: the identity of Jesus; the inner being of God; salvation; mediation; the working of the Holy Spirit. Non-Trinitarian groups have sprouted even from staunch Bible-believing denominations (e.g., Oneness Pentecostals). Denial among influential groups of the divine inspiration of the Old and New Testaments and varying beliefs on what is meant by divine inspiration among those who accept the Bible as the Word of God.
#2 One Authoritative Interpretation Accept and proclaim the interpretation of the apostolic community, which also determined and fixed the canon of the New Testament, and the believers of the first millennium of Christianity.	Touchstones of truth in interpreting Scripture: • Beliefs and practices of Christians of the first three centuries • Teachings held in common by the first Christian thought-leaders (the Fathers), • Definitive doctrinal decrees of the Seven Ecumenical Councils (385-787) • Beliefs enshrined in the Creeds of the Seven Ecumenical Councils The ancient liturgies of Jerusalem, Rome, Antioch, Alexandria and Constantinople.	Organic unity of doctrine on the incarnation of God in Jesus; the Trinity; Mary, the Mother of Jesus; salvation as a gift of grace that can be accepted or rejected; mediation by believers on behalf of each other. This body of teaching has been proclaimed and propagated for twenty centuries despite numerous influential and conflicting worldviews that have come and gone. Proclamation of the Old and New Testaments as the inspired Word of God.

Mary – What the Bible Says

All-Holy	The angel Gabriel greets her with the title *Kecharitomene* which is translated as "completely, perfectly, enduringly endowed with grace." (*A Greek Grammar of the New Testament*)
Mother of God	Elizabeth tells Mary, *"How does this happen to me, that the mother of my Lord should come to me?" (Luke 1:43).* "Lord" here quite clearly refers to "God" because all the other usages of "Lord" in this first chapter of the Gospel of *Luke* concerns Yahweh (God). In *Matthew*, the prophecy in Isaiah is applied to Mary: *"'Behold, the virgin shall be with child and bear a son, and they shall name him Emmanuel,' which means 'God is with us.'" (Matthew* 1:23). Here she is explicitly called the Mother of God-with-us.
Intercessor	*"When the wine ran short, the mother of Jesus said to him, "They have no wine.' [And] Jesus said to her, 'Woman, how does your concern affect me? My hour has not yet come.' His mother said to the servers, 'Do whatever he tells you.'" (John 2:3-5).* Mary interceded with Jesus on behalf of the wedding host and he grants her request although it was not part of the divine timetable. Mary non-verbally knew that Jesus was going to grant her request because she tells the servants to prepare for his instructions. When Jesus says, "My hour has not yet come," he is informing her that he will respond to her intercession when his "hour", the hour of glorification, comes. From Jesus' own words, we see that he is telling his Mother to intercede with him once he has been glorified and is with the Father.
Assumed into Heaven	*"A great sign appeared in the sky, a woman clothed with the sun, with the moon under her feet, and on her head a crown of twelve stars. She was with child … She gave birth to a son, a male child, destined to rule all the nations with an iron rod." (Revelation 12:1,5)* The "woman clothed with the sun," given the language used, is from Heaven. The Son born to her is Jesus the Messiah which means she is Mary.
Mother of All Christians	*"Then the dragon became angry with the woman and went off to wage war against the rest of her offspring, those who keep God's commandments and bear witness to Jesus." (Revelation 12:17).* The Mother of Jesus, Mary, is also the mother of who all bear witness to him and keep the commandments of God.
To be venerated	*"When Elizabeth heard Mary's greeting, the infant leaped in her womb, and Elizabeth, filled with the holy Spirit, cried out in a loud voice and said, "Most blessed are you among women, and blessed is the fruit of your womb. And how does this happen to me, that the mother of my Lord should come to me? For at the moment the sound of your greeting reached my ears, the infant in my womb leaped for joy. Blessed are you who believed that what was spoken to you by the Lord would be fulfilled." And Mary said: … behold, from now on will all ages call me blessed." (Luke 1:41-46,48).* Scripture says that Mary is to be "blessed" because she "believed" and that "all ages" are to call her "blessed." It was at the sound of *her* voice that "the infant … leaped for joy."

The starting-points in our investigation into the Mother of Jesus are twofold:

> *how* we interpret what we find in canonical Scripture and
> *what* we find in canonical Scripture

The *how* and the *what* are inseparable. In this section, we will study both.

We start with the "how" and then move to the "what" because we need the "how" to make sense of the "what."

HOW

Slogans will not help us here. Controversies about "Church vs. Bible" or "Tradition vs. Scripture" simply muddy the waters. There is no such thing as "the Bible alone" simply because our *interpretation of the words* of Scripture is different from *the words themselves*. We need *both* the actual text and our interpretation of the text. And, inevitably, our interpretation is determined by our socio-cultural background and theological assumptions, namely, our "tradition."

Also, by its very nature, any written text can be interpreted in a wide variety of ways. This is the case also with any text that is said to be divinely inspired. Thus, most biblical texts, even those vitally concerned with salvation, have been interpreted in radically different ways.

So, in asking which is the "biblical Mary" we should realize that there are as many versions of the "biblical Mary" as there are readers with differing backgrounds – thousands, if not millions, of different backgrounds. (This is the case not simply with the understanding of Mary but of all Christian affirmations.) But which is the real Mary of Scripture?

There are only two possible answers, two possible approaches, to a question of this kind: either there is no way to determine what is the true interpretation of a scriptural text or there is one authentic interpretation.

In short, either

we can *never know* what is the truth revealed in Scripture
OR
there is one body of truth concerning the authentic
interpretation of Scripture that always remains the same.
We can easily see why these two approaches are the only
two options.

1 No Authoritative Interpretation

Turning to the first authority-denying approach, let us say we
believe the Bible to be an "inerrant" document but do not accept
any authoritative teachings or "traditions" concerning the texts
in the Bible. If we take this approach, then we have no assurance
that we will ever understand what any biblical text *actually* means.
The inevitable consequence is that we can never arrive at their true
interpretation. This is because every key verse in the Bible can be
interpreted in many different ways.

If this prognosis seems extreme, consider the fact that we have
some 45,000+ different Christian denominations with their own
interpretations of scriptural texts (on sanctification, predestination,
music in church, the Trinity, etc.). Some believers might say that the
Holy Spirit will lead them to the true interpretation of the biblical
texts. The problem is that many individuals claim to be led by the
Holy Spirit but have contradictory or varying interpretations of the
very same texts. Believers claiming to be led by the inner testimony
of the Holy Spirit disagree vehemently on all manner of doctrine
from the identity of Jesus to salvation to the Church to eschatology.
So, the claim of being guided by the "inner testimony" of the Spirit
simply leaves us with the same discernment problem we began
with. In short, if we adopt an individual-centered perspective, we
have no way of knowing with any level of certainty the accurate
interpretation of any verse.

If we say we will rely on the "New Testament scholars" for interpreting
biblical texts, we find that these scholars constantly give conflicting

interpretations of the same texts. Worse, the interpretations that are in vogue in one era are dismissed in the next.

After three centuries of intensive effort, New Testament criticism has produced numerous competing hypotheses and hundreds of volumes of speculation. The hypotheses are invariably the objects of fierce dispute and the victims of rapid demise as the attention span of academia turns to the attractions of the next season.

As for the fruits of this approach, Michael Cahill concludes that, "Since Bultmann, progress has been made in the area of the world of Jesus, but not a jot of firm knowledge of the individual historical person of Jesus has been garnered."[1]

Charlotte Allen points out that "The quest for the historical Jesus has produced surprisingly little genuine and uncontroverted new knowledge over the past three centuries about the man and his time. … To this day, nearly our only sources of information about Jesus remain the Gospels and other Christian writings of the first century which have been available for more than 1,900 years."[2]

So, the New Testament theologians are no better than the authority-denying denominations when it comes to providing authoritative interpretations.

2 One Authoritative Interpretation

The only way out of this quandary is the second approach.

But what basis is there for adopting the second approach – the idea that there is a single authentic, authoritative interpretation? And how can we possibly find this binding interpretation? As it applies to our present quest, how can we discover the true biblical Mary?

Actually, the second approach was seen as normal and natural by Christians in the first millennium of Christianity (and after) because they had a clear, universally agreed upon mechanism in place for discerning the inerrant truths revealed by Scripture. The essential element of this mechanism was the authoritative interpretation of the very apostolic community that "produced" and "certified" (under divine inspiration) the books of the New Testament.

By apostolic community, we mean the Christian community of the first 300 years, the community of the Apostles followed by their disciples, the community that existed prior to the finalization of the New Testament canon in the fourth century.

The "interpretation" of the apostolic community was embodied in the liturgies and devotions of the earliest Christians and the body of truth bequeathed by the Elders ("Fathers") and, later, the Councils of the undivided community. This, we might say, is the goose that laid the golden eggs we call doctrines.

Strictly speaking, we should realize that we are dealing not with the "interpretation" of the apostolic community as such but with the proclamation of this community that manifested itself in biblical texts reflecting their faith. In other words, it is not a matter of the texts coming first followed by the "interpretation" of the community. Rather, their perception of events came first, followed by texts that reflected their perception.

The relation of the apostolic community to the books of the New Testament is analogous to the relation between the people of Israel and the books of the Old Testament. During Old Testament times, the Israelities had oral narratives as well as the Ark, the Temple and the Prophets. The Old Testament books manifest the experiences, encounters and perceptions of the Israelites much as the New Testament books reveal the heart and soul of the apostolic community.

Let us not forget that it is this community that selected the canon of New Testament Scripture. There were many gospels and epistles circulating in the first days of Christendom. The apostolic community decided which of these documents were divinely inspired and which were not. The first complete list of all the books of the New Testament is found in the mid-fourth century *Codex Sinaiticus* manuscript. The so-called Gelasian Decretal also lists all the New Testament books. Although its authorship and date of origin is disputed, it is an early (fifth or sixth century) document that testifies to the roles of fourth century and fifth century popes and a fourth century Council of Rome in finalizing the New Testament canon.

Evangelical scholars today admit the role of the apostolic community in setting the canon of Scripture: "The undeniable human element in the history of the canon, and the time factor in the process of canonization all show the human side of the Bible. The canon of Scripture is not a book which fell from heaven."[3]

A key criterion in determining divine inspiration was the question of whether the teachings embedded in a given writing were consistent with the truths proclaimed by the community – and these included the truths they held about Mary. If this community was mistaken in its fundamental teachings, then there is no reason to accept *its authority* in selecting the books that constitute the New Testament. Which means we cannot accept the New Testament unless we first accept the singular authority of the apostolic community with regard to *both* the content of their pre-existing faith and the selection of divinely inspired scripture.

The choice is simple: either the interpretation of biblical texts made by the apostolic community is authoritative and, hence, the only authentic interpretation *OR we cannot even accept the New Testament as Scripture since it is this apostolic community that made the "interpretation" as to which books are divinely inspired and worthy of inclusion in the canon of Scripture.* In fact, as highlighted, they included in the New Testament canon only writings that conformed with their *pre-existing* teaching.

Keep in mind that even if one or more biblical passages appear to contradict an authoritative interpretation of the apostolic community, the burden of proof is in favor of that interpretation. When Jesus says, "The Father is greater than I" (*John* 14:28), this statement should not be seen as contradicting the doctrine that the Three Persons of the Trinity are co-equal. For that matter the doctrine of the Trinity is not spelled out as such in Scripture and its precise formulation took place over centuries despite the problem of certain seemingly inconsistent texts. In fact, every Christian group, if it wishes to be recognized as such, has to maintain a Trinitarian interpretation of Scripture.

Once one doctrine is rejected, others follow. Evangelical Baptist theologian Timothy George writes, "In time, of course, some evangelicals not only threw the virgin Mary overboard, they also abandoned the Holy Trinity. This was especially true in England, where virtually the entire denomination of General or Arminian Baptists converted en masse to Unitarianism."[4]

In the next two sections, we will examine the "interpretation" of the apostolic community of the biblical texts concerning Mary, the mother of Jesus, and thereby discover the "biblical" Mary.

But first we will review the biblical texts relating to Mary.

WHAT

These texts are of three kinds: what Mary says, what is said about her, what we see her doing. We consider each kind in turn.

Her Words

In reading the New Testament, we find very few words uttered by Mary. But every one of these words had momentous consequences in what early Christianity proclaimed to be the divine plan of salvation.

When she said to the angel Gabriel, "Let what you have said be done to me, " the Holy Spirit "came upon" her and she became the Mother of the Redeemer of humanity.

When she greeted her cousin Elizabeth, the Holy Spirit Himself spoke to her through Elizabeth saying that at the sound of Mary's voice, "the child in my womb leaped for joy" – an event that has historically been regarded as the sanctification of John the Baptist in the womb.

When the Spirit-inspired Elizabeth praised her for the act of faith and obedience that caused her to be "blessed," Mary responded with the proclamation of praise we call the Magnificat.

Two things should be noted about this hymn: first, Mary attributes her glorification to God and, second, she says "all generations will call her blessed" because of what God has done for her (and God bestowed this blessing, we find from Elizabeth's statement just before, because Mary "believed"). Those who believe that Scripture is inspired by God will acknowledge that, in proclaiming the divine decree that she is to be called blessed, Mary is not showing a lack of humility. In praising Mary, we are implicitly praising God's infinite generosity and love in working through the humble and the lowly and in richly blessing those who obey Him. Jesus himself has told us not to hide our light under a bushel for, in bearing testimony to the blessing we have received, we bear testimony to God.

Of course, the biblical narratives tell us that Mary is to be praised not for her physical relationship with Jesus but because of her obedience to the divine will – she is blessed because she "believed."

When she questions the missing boy Jesus in the Temple or inquires after him in the midst of the crowds, she is acting as would any mother concerned about her child. Anything less would be less than human.

Finally, in the most famous wedding in history, her Son changes his own timeline for his ministry in response to her words, "They have no wine."

If we consider the actual texts relating to the wedding of Cana, we see the following:

- Mary asked Jesus to perform a miracle, in this case replenish the wine that had run out.

- Seemingly refusing this request, Jesus said "My hour has not yet come" (*John* 2:4)

- Mary does not respond but asks the servants Do whatever he tells you." (*John* 2:5)

- Jesus asks the servers to fill the jars with water and take them to the headwaiter. On tasting the water that has been turned into wine, the headwaiter tells the bridegroom, "you have kept the good wine until now." (*John* 2:10)

- This was the first of Jesus' signs as a result of which his disciples begin to believe in him.

- What is obvious from these texts is the following

  o Mary interceded with Jesus on behalf of the wedding host and he grants her request although it was not part of the divine timetable.

  o Mary non-verbally knew that Jesus was going to grant her request because she tells the servants to prepare for his instructions

  o When Jesus says, "My hour has not yet come," he is informing her that he will respond to her intercession when his "hour" comes. What does he mean by "my hour"? In *John* 17, we read "When Jesus had said this, he raised his eyes to heaven and said, "Father, the hour has come. Give glory to your son, so that your son may glorify you … And now I will no longer be in the world, but they are in the world, while I am coming to you." (17:1,11). Ralph Russell writes, "The implication of [*John* 2:4] is that when his 'hour' has come, and 'hour' in St. John is the hour of his passion and glorification, it will be different. Yet Mary knows he will do something now for the young couple and says to the servants 'do whatever he tells you.'"[5] From Jesus' own words, we see that he is telling his Mother to intercede with him once he has been glorified and is with the Father.

Words About Her

Kecharitomene – "Our tainted nature's solitary boast"

Mother! whose virgin bosom was uncrost
With the least shade of thought to sin allied;
Woman! above all women glorified,
Our tainted nature's solitary boast.
William Wordsworth, "The Virgin"

One of the most stunning statements in the entire Bible is the Angel Gabriel's greeting to Mary in the Gospel of *Luke*. He greets her not by her name but with a title. It is a Greek word, *"kecharitomene."* It is a word used nowhere else in the Bible – thus signifying the uniqueness of the recipient. Its meaning is clear. German Protestant linguist Friedrich Blass, in his classic work *A Greek Grammar of the New Testament* (updated by Albert Debrunner), writes that on "Greek grammatical and linguistic grounds" the phrase means "completely, perfectly, enduringly endowed with grace."[6] Although the greeting has been translated in a variety of ways ranging from

"Hail full of grace" to "Rejoice so highly favored" what is important is not what various translations say (given the difficulty of adequately communicating unique senses) but what the phrase means in the original Greek. On this, there is no dispute.

Greek scholar A.T. Robertson, a Baptist, notes that "kecharitomene" is the "perfect passive participle of charitoo and means endowed with grace (charis)."[7] The transformation by grace is a permanent condition and not a transitory event. Herbert Weir Smyth, professor of Greek at Harvard University, wrote that the perfect past participle "denotes a completed action the effects of which still continue in the present."[8]

What is especially significant is this: Scripture tells us that she was transformed by divine grace even before the coming of Christ. But what is meant by "grace" in the New Testament? It is the freely given Life of God, the sanctifying divine action in our being necessary for salvation:

> "For by grace you have been saved through faith, and this is not from you; it is the gift of God." (*Ephesians* 2:8)
> "All have sinned and are deprived of the glory of God. They are justified freely by his grace through the redemption in Christ Jesus. (*Romans* 3:23-4)
> "He saved us through the bath of rebirth and renewal by the holy Spirit, whom he richly poured out on us through Jesus Christ our savior, so that we might be justified by his grace and become heirs in hope of eternal life." (*Titus* 3:5-7)
> "For if by that one person's transgression the many died, how much more did the grace of God and the gracious gift of the one person Jesus Christ overflow for the many." (*Romans* 5:15).

Since the presence of grace in a person or persons is used in different contexts in the New Testament, we return to *kecharitomene*. Although this phrase is found nowhere else, its root, *charitoo*, as it pertains to grace, is found one other time in the New Testament, in the epistle to the *Ephesians* 1:6 (albeit not in the same complete and permanent sense as *kecharitomene*). The verses preceding it give the context for verse 6 which is italicized here:

> "Blessed be the God and Father of our Lord Jesus Christ, who has blessed us in Christ with every spiritual blessing in the heavens, as he chose us in him, before the foundation of the world, to be holy and without blemish before him. In love he destined us for adoption to himself through Jesus Christ, in accord with the favor of his will, *for the praise of the glory of his grace that he granted us in the beloved.*" (*Ephesians* 1:3-6).

But in *Ephesians* the phrase is applied to Christians who have been redeemed by the Blood of Christ through baptism. When applied to Mary, however, Jesus had not yet been born. So how could she have been thus transformed? This is precisely where the ancient Christian understanding of Mary's preservation from sin makes sense.

In delving further into the meaning of *kecharitomene*, the exegete Ignace de la Potterie writes:

> As has been shown in a study on the history of that word, the dominant translation which ancient Christianity has given is very clear: the Byzantine tradition in the East and the medieval tradition in the West have seen in "kecharitomene," the indication of Mary's perfect holiness. . . .

> The verb utilized here by Luke (charitoun) is extremely rare in Greek. It is present only two times in the New Testament: in the text of Luke on the Annunciation (Lk 1:28) " kecharitomene," and in the Epistle to the Ephesians (Eph 1:6), "echaritosen." . . .

These verbs, then, effect a change of something in the person or the thing affected. Thus, the radical of the verb "charitoo" being "charis" (=grace), the idea which is expressed is that of a change brought about by grace. In addition, the verb used by Luke is in the past perfect participial form. "Kecharitomene" signifies then, in the person to whom the verb relates, that is, Mary, that the action of the grace of God has already brought about a change. It does not tell us how that came about. What is essential here, is that it affirms that Mary has been transformed by the grace of God. …

The verb used by Luke is in the past perfect participial form. "Kecharitomene" signifies then, in the person to whom the verb relates, that is, Mary, that the action of the grace of God has already brought about a change. …

In what then would this transformation of grace consist? According to the parallel text of the Letter to the Ephesians 1 :6 the Christians have been "transformed by grace" in the sense that "according to the richness of his grace, they find redemption by his blood, the remission of sins" (Eph 1 :7). This grace, in reality, takes away sin. This is elucidating for our particular case. Mary is "transformed by grace," because she has been sanctified by the grace of God. It is there, moreover, in the Church's tradition that we have the most customary translation. Sophronius of Jerusalem, for example, interprets the term "full of grace" in this manner: "No one has been fully sanctified as you ...: no one has been purified in advance as you." In addition, he takes from the total context that Mary had been "transformed by the grace" of God in view of the task which she awaits, that of becoming the Mother of the Son of God, and to do so while remaining a virgin. There we have the double announcement of the angel: as mother she brings to the world the Son of the Most High (v. 33), but that will take place by the "power of the Most High" (v. 35), that is, virginally. God had prepared Mary for this by inspiring in her

> the desire for virginity (see below v. 34). This desire of Mary was then for her a result of her transformation by grace. …
>
> It is true that we do not find in the text of Luke evidence that Mary is "full of grace" from the first moment of her existence. But what in reality does the proclamation of the dogma of the Immaculate Conception say? Grace has preserved Mary of all sin and of all consequences of sin (concupiscence). This is also the biblical understanding of the concept of "grace." Grace takes away sin (Eph 1:6- 7). If it is true that Mary was entirely transformed by the grace of God, that then means that God has preserved her from sin, "purified" her, and sanctified her. …
>
> As one can notice in the schema of the structured text the theme of "being full of grace" is continued in the first proclamation, "You have found grace with God!'; then follows the substance of the announcement: Mary will become the mother of the Messiah. It is apparent that Mary was full of grace by God in view of this maternity, and even that she was prepared, by the grace of her virginity, for her own mission, that of being the virginal mother of the Savior."[9]

Polemicists have tried to downplay the relevance of the phrase to doctrine. Some have said that the Church's first martyr Stephen too was called "full of grace" but, as scholars point out, the Greek word in that verse (*pleres charitos*) is used as an adjective and not a noun and concerns grace given at that moment (after he had become a Christian) and not a grace that is a past and permanent condition as with *kecharitomene.* As la Potterie writes, *kecharitomene* is used in the "the past perfect participial form" as in "one who has always been filled with grace."

Whether the phrase is translated as "highly favored" or "full of grace" (neither of which capture all that is being said), the meaning of the phrase is to be sought in the original Greek formulation, *kecharitomene.* It might be asked, how should we interpret the application of *kecharitomene* to Mary?

Here, what is decisive is not an opinion poll of today's exegetes and theologians. Rather, we should only consider what Greek-speaking Christians understood it to mean in the ancient Church. The meaning of a word is to be sought in its usage by native speakers of the period in question not in speculation emanating from centuries and societies far removed. When we explore the meaning of the phrase from this standpoint, we find that the millennia-old interpretation of the phrase is the only available option.

As the great Greek Fathers and Byzantine hymns saw it, the angel's greeting to the Virgin referred to her lifelong state of grace and freedom from sin.

John Chrysostom's paean of praise specifically centers on *kecharitomene*:

> *Hail, Kecharitomene, faultless one carrying the immutable divinity. … Hail, Kecharitomene, habitation of holy fire. … Hail, Kecharitomene, interminable grace of the holy virgin. … Hail, Kecharitomene, golden urn, contaning heavenly manna.*[10]

As we shall see in the next section, the Greek Fathers before and after Chrysostom, as well as the Latin and Syriac Fathers, bear witness to the holy and sinless state of the biblical Mary.

The Greek-speaking Origen (185-254 AD) in his commentary remarks on the uniqueness of the phrase:

> "Because the angel greeted Mary with new expressions, which I have never encountered elsewhere in the Scriptures, it is necessary to comment on this. I do not, in fact, recall having read in any other place in the Sacred Scriptures these words: Rejoice, O Full of Grace. Neither of these expressions is ever addressed to a man: such a special greeting was reserved only for Mary."[11]

We might note in passing that, in the Bible, people who are soon to play a key part in salvation history have a name change given by God signifying their future roles. For instance, Abram becomes Abraham "father of nations" and Jacob becomes Israel. Mary becomes the embodiment of God's free gift of grace, the only human person "enduringly endowed with grace." This is appropriate indeed because she is soon to become *Theotokos*, the God-bearer.

"The Mother of My Lord"

"*Theotokos*," "God-bearer," "Mother of God," is the first defined title of Mary. It was declared as definitive Christian doctrine at the Council of Ephesus in 431 A.D.

Long before the definition, however, the Gospels made it clear that she was indeed the God-bearer. Elizabeth ("filled with the Holy Spirit") exclaims, "How does this happen to me, that the mother of my Lord should come to me?" (*Luke* 1:43). "Lord" here quite clearly refers to "God" because all the other usages of "Lord" in this first chapter of the Gospel of Luke concerns Yahweh (God):

"Observing all the commandments and ordinances of the Lord blamelessly" (1:6);

"He was chosen by lot to enter the sanctuary of the Lord" (1:9);

"the angel of the Lord" (1: 11).

About this passage, biblical scholar Brant Pitre writes, "Both Jewish and Christian scholars agree that, in context, Elizabeth's use of 'Lord' refers to Jesus' kingship and his divine identity. If this is correct, then the New Testament identification of Mary as the 'mother' (Greek *meter*) of the 'Lord' (Greek *kyrios*) provides a biblical foundation for the Church's teaching that Mary is also the 'Mother of God.'"

Pitre then asks us to consider the infancy narrative in *Matthew*. "Look closely again at the Gospel of Matthew: "'Behold, the virgin shall be with child and *bear* (Greek *tikto*) a son, and they shall name him Emmanuel,' which means '*God* (Greek *theos*) is with us.'" (Matthew 1:23) There it is right there on the first page of the New Testament! Mary is the virgin who will "bear" (Greek *tikto*) the child who is *God* (*theos*) with us. In other words, Mary is the 'God-bearer' (Greek *Theo-tokos*)! It is no wonder that it was ancient Greek-speaking Christians who came up with this title for Mary. They were reading the New Testament in the original Greek – not in translation. And they were reading it in light of the Old Testament."[12]

We should also note that Jesus' human body is the body not of a creature but of God. Mary is the Mother of "Emmanuel," "God-is-with-us."

"A Woman Clothed with the Sun"

"When Jesus saw his mother and the disciple there whom he loved, he said to his mother, "Woman, behold, your son." Then he said to the disciple, "Behold, your mother." And from that hour the disciple took her into his home." *John 19:26-7*

"A great sign appeared in the sky, a woman clothed with the sun, with the moon under her feet, and on her head a crown of twelve stars. She was with child … Then the dragon stood before the woman about to give birth, to devour her child when she gave birth. She gave birth to a son, a male child, destined to rule all the nations with an iron rod. Her child was caught up to God and his throne. … The huge dragon, the ancient serpent, who is called the Devil and Satan, who deceived the whole world, was thrown down to earth, and its angels were thrown down with it. Then I heard a loud voice in heaven say … "The Devil has come down to you in great fury, for he knows he has but a short time." When the dragon saw that it had been thrown down to the earth, it pursued the woman who had given birth to the male child.. … Then the dragon became angry with the woman and went off to wage war against the rest of her offspring, those who keep God's commandments and bear witness to Jesus." *Revelation* 1-2,4-5, 9-10,12-13, 17

The Gospels spotlight the role played by Mary in the earthly mission of her Son. The Gospel of *John* and the *Book of Revelation* tell us that this role takes on a new dimension in the work of salvation through the rest of history. We learn in the Epistles that those who accept the divine offer of salvation become adopted brothers and sisters of Jesus filled with the Holy Spirit and thereby children of the Abba Father. But to become an adopted brother or sister of Jesus is to become a child of his Mother. This last feature tells us why her Son tells his beloved disciple, "Behold, your mother."

As Brant Pitre and other New Testament scholars have pointed out, the "beloved disciple" in John represents all disciples. "The Beloved Disciple represents every disciple" and so "Jesus is also giving Mary to all who believe in him—all his "beloved disciples."[13]

The *Book of Revelation* consolidates the understanding that all the followers of Jesus become children of his Mother. *Revelation* 12 spells out her divinely appointed role – to be our Mother.

Taken as it stands, there can be little doubt that the Woman Clothed with the Sun is Mary, the Mother of Jesus. For the text says earlier that she is the mother of "a son … destined to rule all the nations with an iron rod.". This is a reference to Psalm 2 with its prophecy of the Messiah who will rule all nations with an iron rod. From the reference to the Messianic Psalm 2 and to the account of his ascension to Heaven (*Revelation* 12:5), it is apparent that the son of the Woman is Jesus.

Strangely, many of today's most ardent defenders of the literal reading of Scripture have suddenly developed cold feet concerning the literal truth of this passage. Yes, they say, the text shows that she is the Mother of the Messiah but we should interpret "Mother" to mean the People of Israel or, if that does not work, as the Christian Church. Neither of these allegorical interpretations "work" for various reasons. You cannot justify a collective interpretation of one of the figures (the Woman) and an individual interpretation for the other (the Son). Second, the people of Israel have never been represented as the Mother of an individual who is the Messiah anywhere else in Scripture. In fact, the writer of *Revelation* is painfully aware of the persecution of Christians by the enemies of Jesus and it is unimaginable that he would represent them playing a maternal role! Third, the Christian Church cannot seriously be thought of as the "mother" of Christ when the Church emerges *from* Christ. In fact, the Woman is shown as Mother of all Christians. So, the Marian interpretation is the only plausible one.

Of course, Mary, the Mother of the Messiah, in her own being represents both the People of Israel and the Church and thus, in a secondary allegorical sense, the "Woman" can be seen as representing both Israel and the Church. For an example, think of the references to the Daughter of Zion in the Old Testament that parallel texts about the Mary of the New Testament. At a primary level, "Daughter of Zion" referred to Israel but in a secondary sense, it has been seen as a prophecy of the Virgin Mary who embodies Israel receiving her Savior.

Pitre explains that since both the Child (Jesus) and the Dragon (the Devil) are concrete individuals, the woman too has to be seen as an individual. And since she is shown to be the Mother of the Child, she is none other than the Virgin Mary. He notes too that, since she is wearing a crown, the Woman is a queen and, in view of the practice in ancient Israel, she has to be seen as the Queen-Mother. The Mother who is thereby Queen.[14]

Evangelical biblical scholar Ben Witherington writes, "This *figure* [the Woman of *Revelation* 12] is both the literal mother of the male child Jesus and also the female image of the people of God."[15]

At its close, *Revelation* 12 has more to tell us about the Woman: "Then the dragon became angry with the woman and went off to wage war against the rest of her offspring, those who keep God's commandments and bear witness to Jesus."

As the text makes clear, all those who "bear witness for Jesus", then, are children of the Woman. As we have seen, the Woman is the Mother of Jesus. The dragon is referenced (12:9) to "the primeval serpent known as the devil or Satan" of *Genesis* 3. *Revelation* 12 is thus linked to *Genesis* 3 which refers to the future conflict between the serpent and the Woman and her Son.

Historically, Christians (including Martin Luther) have seen *Genesis* 3 as a prophecy of the coming of Christ and his Mother and their war with Satan. This dovetails with the *Revelation* 12 account of the war between Christ and his Mother on the one side and Satan on the other. The International Ecumenical Bible Commentary notes that *Revelation* 12:17 is a clear reference to the messianic text of *Genesis* 3:15. Pitre writes that

> the oldest Jewish interpretations that we possess of the biblical oracle about the "serpent" and the "woman" (*Genesis* 3:15) saw it as a prophecy of the Messiah. The most significant example of this is the book of Enoch, which was very popular among Jews of the first century A.D. This ancient Jewish writing not only identifies the 'Messiah' with the 'Son of Man' (1 Enoch 48:2-10) but also links the Son of Man with the prophecy of the woman in Genesis 3:15:
>
> > Pain shall seize them when they see that *Son of Man* sitting on the throne of his glory ... For *the offspring of the mother of the living* was concealed from the beginning. (1 Enoch 62:5-7)
>
> What a remarkable passage! It shows us that already in the

first century A.D., the Jewish messiah was being identified with the 'offspring' of Eve, the mother of all living (Genesis 3:15, 22).[16]

Mary's Motherhood as manifested in *Revelation* 12 shows her mediation on behalf of her children.

Her Acts

The importance that Mary's words have in Scripture are matched by the importance attributed to her acts at key events in the biblical narrative:

- She is fundamental to the Incarnation because it she who gave birth to Immanuel;
- at the presentation in the Temple, the Holy Spirit inspires Simeon to say to Mary that, when her Son is rejected, "a sword will pierce your own soul too";
- her Son first speaks to her of his mission at the Temple – "'Did you not know that I must be in my Father's house?' … and his mother kept all these things in her heart";
- at Calvary, her Son establishes her as mother of all believers, "This is your mother";
- at the birth of the Church, the author of *Acts* notes that "the mother of Jesus" is present when the Holy Spirit descends on all the believers gathered in prayer;
- and in *Revelation* 12 we are given the glorious vision of her as the mother of all those "who obey God's commandments and bear witness for Jesus."

When you couple the impact of the words from her and about her in the biblical narratives with her presence at key salvation-events, it should be apparent that Mary, the Mother of Jesus, plays a role in the salvific sequence second only to her Son. Her Son's role is infinite in scope. Hers' is the highest at the finite level.

#2 WHAT THE NEW TESTAMENT APOSTOLIC COMMUNITY PROCLAIMED

New Eve, Queen-Mother, Mother of Emmanuel, All-Holy Ark of the Covenant, Intercessory Mother of the Faithful, Virgin Mary

Mary – What the New Testament Apostolic Community Proclaimed

Role	Fathers	Liturgies	Devotions
New Eve	✓	✓	✓
Queen Mother	✓	✓	✓
Mother of Emmanuel	✓	✓	✓
All-Holy Ark of the Covenant	✓	✓	✓
Intercessory Mother of the Faithful	✓	✓	✓
Virgin	✓	✓	✓

We turn now to the real "biblical Mary" – that is to say, Mary as understood, perceived and proclaimed by the apostolic community. This community includes the Apostles and their disciples as well as the faithful of the first 300 years of the first Christian millennium who preserved and propagated the faith before the fixing of the canon of the New Testament and the coming together of the first Ecumenical Council.

We have considered the texts that speak of the Mother of Jesus in the New Testament – the encounters with the angel Gabriel and her cousin Elizabeth, the birth of her Son and his presentation in the Temple, the finding of her Son in the Temple, the wedding feast at Cana, the vigil at Calvary, the prayer with the Apostles before Pentecost and, finally, her appearance as Mother of all Christians.

Collectively, just as the books of the Old Testament were preceded by an oral tradition that was later reduced to writing, the texts of the New Testament that speak of Mary were preceded by the oral tradition of the apostolic community. The biblical texts mirror this oral tradition of the apostolic community.

BEFORE the fixing of the canon of the New Testament, the apostolic community proclaimed Mary to be the New Eve, the Queen-Mother, the intercessory Mother of all Christians, the Theotokos (Mother of God), the Panagia (the All-Holy – the feminine form of "Panagion" which was the term used to describe the Holy Spirit), the Aeiparthenos (Ever-Virgin). The last three titles were, in fact, declared as essential elements of the Christian Faith by Councils accepted by all Christians.

Even a critic of Marian devotion like the Baptist Albert Mohler acknowledged that "forms of Marian devotion *can be traced to the earliest periods of church history.*"[1]

About this early history, John F. Murphy writes, "In the historical narrative of the New Testament Mary habitually appears in the Gospel scene in circumstances which reveal her unique association with Christ and His work, and significantly indicate her position of singular importance. Especially St. Luke pondered over the association of Christ and His Mother and the sublimity of her vocation. The simple and seemingly incidental references to Mary in the New Testament in general are of such nature as to indicate that the contemporary eyewitnesses of Gospel times would necessarily have felt personal love and veneration for Our Lady. … Consequently, the point must be made that the historical and theological foundations upon which the framework of Marian devotion rests were actually laid in the first century. To deny this is to discount the fact of Mary's presence in the early Church. 'All these with one mind continued steadfastly in prayer with the women and Mary, the mother of Jesus.'"[2]

What this means is that the Mary proclaimed by the apostolic community was not an "interpretation" of Scripture. Rather, *it was a divinely-granted vision collectively experienced and encountered by the first Christians that was represented in and by Scripture. This "collective consciousness" was inextricably embedded in the faith of the martyrs and evangelists.*

We shall consider each of the five dimensions of the proclamation/vision/collective consciousness in turn.

The New Eve

Mary's "Yes" to God's invitation to be the Mother of his Son was the pivotal act of her life as was recognized from the start. This is precisely why the first, unanimous and single most important teaching of the apostolic community about Mary is that she is the New Eve. The earliest and the later of the great thought-leaders of the Christian Church, the Fathers, consistently proclaimed this truth. The Church Fathers –whose unanimous expositions of Christian truth have been taken as normative by generations of Christians, Protestant, Catholic and Orthodox – belonged to three eras, the era of the Apostles, the era before the Council of Nicaea held in 325 (ante-Nicene) and the era after this Council (post-Nicene).

The Fathers, starting with Justin the Martyr, 100-165 A.D., saw an inverse parallelism in the contrast between Adam and Eve and Jesus and Mary. As the evil angel seduces Eve to disobey God, and Eve in turn persuades Adam to open the doors of damnation, so a good angel comes to Mary with a divine command that she obeys and thus gives birth to the Jesus who opens the doors to redemption. Hence, she is the New Eve while Jesus is the New Adam.

The contrast between Eve and Mary, Adam and Christ, the evil angel in Eden and the good angel at the Annunciation, and the Tree of the Knowledge of Good and Evil and the Tree of the Cross, lies at the heart of the history of salvation.

This is the hidden and yet obvious truth in Scripture that became foundational to the theology and devotional life of the first Christians. Scholars today point out that Justin's understanding of the Virgin Mary is taken exclusively from Scripture. The distinguished Lutheran (and later Orthodox) church historian

Jaroslav Pelikan observes that Fathers like Irenaeus, when writing about Mary as the New Eve, do not even try to argue for this interpretation since it was already considered a part of the basic body of Christian belief.

The history of salvation in the Judeo-Christian revelation is built around covenants between God and humanity. The idea of a covenant entails an agreement freely entered into by two parties, on the one side God and on the other humanity. Pelikan tells us that, in the Christian vision, two of the key players on the human side were Eve and Mary.[3]

This is the message of the Fathers as illustrated in the citations below.[4]

Take first the Fathers of the second and third centuries.

Justin Martyr (100-165)
> "He became man by the Virgin in order that the disobedience which proceeded from the serpent might receive its destruction in the same manner in which it derived its origin. For Eve, who was a virgin and undefiled, having conceived by the word of the serpent brought forth disobedience and death. But the Virgin Mary received faith and joy, when the angel Gabriel announced the good tidings to her that the Spirit of the Lord would come upon her, and the power of the Most High would overshadow her, wherefore also the Holy One begotten of her is the Son of God, and she replied, 'Be it done unto me according to your word.'" (*Dialogue with Trypho*).

Irenaeus of Lyons (140-202):
> "[Eve] having become disobedient, was made the cause of death, both to herself and to the entire human race; so also did Mary, having a man betrothed [to her], and being nevertheless a virgin, by yielding obedience, become the

cause of salvation, both to herself and the whole human race." (*Against Heresies III*).

"And just as it was through a virgin who disobeyed that man was stricken and fell and died, so too it was through the Virgin, who obeyed the word of God, that man resuscitated by life received life. ... Adam was necessarily to be restored in Christ, that mortality be absorbed in immortality, and Eve in Mary, that a virgin, become the advocate of a virgin, should undo and destroy virginal disobedience by virginal obedience." (*Proof of the Apostolic Teaching*).

Tertullian (155-240):

"God recovered His image and likeness in a procedure similar to that in which He had been robbed of it by the devil. For it was while Eve was still a virgin that the word of the devil crept in to erect an edifice of death. Likewise, through a Virgin, the Word of God was introduced to set up a structure of life." "As Eve had believed the serpent, so Mary believed the angel. The delinquency which the one occasioned by believing, the other by believing effaced." (*The Flesh of Christ*).

The same teaching is proclaimed by the Fathers of the fourth and fifth centuries.

Athanasius of Alexandria (295-373)

"Eve listened to the suggestion of the serpent and tribulation descended upon all. And you have inclined your ears to the supplications of Gabriel, and penitence flourished." (*De Virginitate*).

Ephrem of Syria (306-373)

"Eve brought on the sin, and the debt was reserved for the Virgin Mary, that she might pay the debts of her mother, and tear up the handwriting under which were groaning all generations." (*On the Annunciation of the Mother of God*).

Cyril of Jerusalem (315-386)

"Through Eve yet virgin came death, through a virgin, or rather from a virgin, must Life appear; that as the serpent beguiled the one, so to the other Gabriel might bring good tidings." (*De Christo Incarnato*).

Ambrose of Milan (339-397)

"It was through a man and a woman that flesh was cast from paradise; it was through a virgin that flesh was linked to God." (*Epistle 63*). "Eve is called mother of the human race, but Mary mother of salvation." (*Sermon 45*).

Augustine of Hippo (354-430)

"The first man, by persuasion of a virgin, fell; the Second Man, with consent of a Virgin, triumphed. By a woman the devil brought in death; by a woman the Lord brought in life. An evil angel of old seduced Eve, a good angel likewise encouraged Mary. ... What Eve did by her ill-believing, Mary by her good-believing blotted out. From a woman was the beginning of sin, and on her account we all die, from a woman was the beginning of faith, and on her account are we repaired unto everlasting life." (*Sermon 28*).

Peter Chrysologus (400-450)

"Why Christ wanted to be born is this; that just as death came to all through Eve, so through Mary life might return to all." (*Sermon 99*).

Hesychius of Jerusalem (d. circa 451),

"See how great and of what kind is the dignity of the Virgin Mother of God? For the Only begotten Son of God the world's Creator was born as an infant of her, re-formed Adam, sanctified Eve, drove out the dragon, and opened Paradise, keeping sure the seal of her womb." (*Oratio de Deiparae Laudibus*).

Amphilochilis of Iconium (circa 340-394):
> "Woman was defended by woman, the first opened the way to sin, the present one served to open the way to justice. The former followed the advice of the serpent, the latter brought forth the slayer of the serpent and brought to light the author of light. The former introduced sin through the tree, the latter brings in grace through the tree." (*Patrologia Graeca*, 46).

Two of the most noted historians of the early Christian community – both of them Protestants – pointed to the centrality of Mary as the New Eve in the ancient faith.

Oxford historian J. N. D. Kelly writes:
> The real contribution of these early centuries, however, was more positively theological, and consisted in representing Mary as the antithesis of Eve and drawing out the implications of this. Justin was the pioneer, although the way he introduced the theme suggests that he was not innovating . . . Tertullian and Irenaeus were quick to develop these ideas. The latter, in particular, argued [Against Heresies, 3, 22, 4; cf. 5, 19, 1] that Eve, while still a virgin, had proved disobedient and so became the cause of death both for herself and for all mankind, but Mary, also a virgin, obeyed and became the cause of salvation both for herself and for all mankind. "Thus, as the human race was bound fast to death through a virgin, so through a virgin it was saved." Irenaeus further hinted both at her universal motherhood and at her cooperation in Christ's saving work, describing [Ibid, 4, 33, 1] her womb as "that pure womb which regenerates men to God."[5]

This same point had been made by the 19th century historian and founder of the Evangelical Alliance Philip Schaff:
> Justin Martyr, Irenaeus, and Tertullian, are the first who

> present Mary as the counterpart of Eve, as a "mother
> of all living" in the higher, spiritual sense, and teach
> that she became through her obedience the mediate or
> instrumental cause of the blessings of redemption to the
> human race, as Eve by her disobedience was the fountain
> of sin and death.[6]

The Mary-Eve typology was not just a theological metaphor. It entered into the liturgical celebrations and devotion of the early Christians and became a part of all the ancient liturgies. It was in effect a fundamental Christian teaching that underlies all the doctrines that we call Marian – for instance, she who played an integral role in bringing about the reversal of the effects of Original Sin cannot consistently be thought of as being subject to these effects (for instance, being conceived in sin or suffering bodily corruption).

Moreover, the importance of the Annunciation – of Mary's Yes – for human salvation was not highlighted simply by theologians and pastors. It served as one of the central and persistent themes of artistic creation inspired by the Christian story. Almost all the greatest artists of Christendom have made their own contributions to the depiction of the Annunciation.

Of course, it was clear to all that Mary's role in salvation history did not end with the Annunciation. On the one hand, she is permanently the New Eve just as her Son will always be the New Adam. On the other, we see that she is mysteriously present with the New Adam at precisely the times most crucial to the accomplishment of Redemption. When she offers up her infant Son at the Temple, it is prophesied that a sword will pierce her soul. This prophecy was fulfilled, said the Fathers and the faithful, when her offering came to a climax on Calvary and she became for all time the Sorrowful Mother. The consent given at the Annunciation extended through the Presentation at the Temple to the Sacrifice on Calvary.

As Eve was linked with Adam at all stages of the Fall, so also the New Eve was linked with the New Adam at every step of the road to Redemption. The Fathers recognized that the Incarnation cannot be separated from the Cross and Redemption and in calling Mary the New Eve they drew our attention to the singular role she played in the Redemptive Mission of God Incarnate.

Further, the parallelism of Adam and Eve and Christ and Mary does not cease with their individual acts of obedience and disobedience. These acts had cosmic effects. With the Original Sin of Adam (caused by Eve) the human race and all of creation were thrown into decay and destruction. With the redemptive death of Christ (in which his Mother sorrowfully participated as Simeon had described), the human race and all of creation were called to enter a new splendor even greater than the perfection present before the Fall when everything is brought together "under Christ, as head, everything in the heavens and everything on earth." (*Ephesians* 1:10).

The Christian message is that God does not lose, that his plans always bear fruit. If humanity fell through a man and a woman, humanity would be saved through a man and a woman. If Adam and Eve left the Eden that God had planned for them and their progeny, then the new Adam and the new Eve would take their offspring into a new Eden infinitely more joyous than the first Eden for here all of creation is transformed by the very life of God.

In the Christian dispensation, all of human history is moving inexorably toward this great climactic consummation when "all things [are] to be reconciled through him [Christ] and for him, everything in heaven and everything on earth." (*Colossians* 1:19-20). And as Mary brought Christ into the world in his first coming and suffered with him to the end, she likewise, as Queen-Mother (see below), prepares the way for his coming Reign as King when the divine Will is to be done on earth as it is in Heaven.

The Jewish Queen-Mother in Scripture and Ancient Christianity

Our first glimpse of the biblical Mary is in the Gospels. Mary of Nazareth is Jewish like her Son and his disciples and the earliest leaders of the new Faith. Too often, we have forgotten this in the case of both the Virgin and her Son.

Perhaps the greatest breakthrough in biblical studies over the last three decades has been the discovery of the Jewish Jesus. A May 2008 *Time* story described this as one of the "ten ideas that are changing the world." To understand what Jesus of Nazareth said and did and how he was perceived we must understand first the theological thought-world and symbol-universe in which he lived, spoke and acted. He was Jewish and lived in the world of Second Temple Judaism. Now this might seem obvious but incredibly most of the leading lights in the history of New Testament criticism seemed entirely oblivious to it. As a result they created a Jesus of their own imagination and in their image – a German Jesus or a hippie Jesus, to give two examples, instead of the Jewish Jesus of first century Palestine. They missed the meaning of his affirmations, teachings and actions as understood by his contemporaries. Fortunately, a re-discovery of the Jewish Jesus is now in progress.

In like manner, many Christians today have also ignored the Jewish identity of the Mother of Jesus, Mary of Nazareth. Of central importance here is the understanding of the first Christians – formed by their Jewish legacy – that she was the New Eve, the Queen-Mother and the Ark of the Covenant.

The process of re-discovering the Jewish Mary has finally begun. *Jesus and the Jewish Roots of Mary* by the New Testament scholar Brant Pitre (repeatedly cited here) is a pioneering work in this area. Pitre says, "Judaism is especially important for understanding Mary. … Every book on Mary that rejected Catholic beliefs as unbiblical invariably ignored the Old Testament background of what the New Testament says about Mary. … The reason so many people can't see how biblical Catholic beliefs about Mary really are is because they are only looking at what the New Testament says about her, and ignoring the prefigurations of Mary in the Old Testament. Keep looking at the New Testament in isolation, and you'll never understand who Mary really is. Start looking at Mary through ancient Jewish eyes, and everything becomes clear."[7]

Among other things, in his writings, Pitre highlights the importance for the first Christians of the Virgin's status as Queen-Mother:

> The first Christians did not get their beliefs about Mary from the celestial goddesses of paganism. "It got them from Judaism. In order to see this clearly, you have to look at Mary through ancient Jewish eyes. You have to look at Mary in light of what the Old Testament says about the Jewish Queen.

> In ancient Israel, the king did not rule alone. There was also a queen. However, the queen was not the king's wife, but his mother. She was known as the "Queen Mother"—in Hebrew, the *gebirah*.

> To get an idea of just how important the Queen Mother was, consider what the Bible says about Bathsheba, the wife of King David and mother of King Solomon.

> When Bathsheba comes into David's presence, she bows to him as her king (1 Kings 1:15-16). But after David dies and Solomon her son becomes king, the tables are turned. Now, when Bathsheba comes into Solomon's presence, he bows to her (1 Kings 2:19)! The king himself honors his mother because she is queen.

> But it doesn't stop there. King Solomon also has a "throne" brought in, so that his mother can sit at his "right" hand (1

Kings 2:19). Everyone knew what this meant. The Queen Mother was the most powerful person in the kingdom—second only to the king himself.

That's why when the Queen Mother asks a favor of Solomon, he answers: "Make your request, my mother, for I will not refuse you" (1 Kings 2:20).

What does all this mean for who Mary was, and how Christians see her today?

First, if Jesus really was the long-awaited Jewish King—the Messiah—then his mother was the Jewish Queen.

That's what it would have meant to a Jewish girl like Mary when the angel Gabriel told her that her son would "sit on the throne of his father David" (Luke 1:33). As mother of the new King, Mary would be the new Queen Mother.

It's also why the book of Revelation describes the mother of the Messiah as a woman "in heaven" wearing "a crown of twelve stars" (Revelation 12:1-2). The crown shows she is a queen, and the twelve stars symbolize the people of Israel.

Second, if Mary is the new Queen Mother, then it makes sense to honor her. After all, "Honor your father and your mother" is one of the Ten Commandments (Exodus 20:12). It isn't idolatry to honor the queen. If the queens of earthly kingdoms are honored and loved by their people, then how much more the Queen Mother of the Kingdom of God?

Finally, if Mary is the Queen Mother of Jesus' Kingdom, then she is certainly no ordinary woman. She is, quite literally, the most powerful woman in the universe. She is the true Queen of Heaven.

And Mary is still alive in heaven. (After all, we call it

"eternal life"—not death.). As Queen Mother, Mary sits at Jesus' right hand. And, like King Solomon, Jesus will not refuse her requests.

That's why, since ancient times, Christians have asked Mary to pray for them. Consider the words of the most ancient Christian prayer to Mary we possess, written in Greek and discovered in the early 20th century on a scrap of papyrus:

"Under your mercy, we take refuge, O Mother of God. Do not disregard our prayers in time of trouble, but deliver us from danger, O only pure one, only blessed one." (Anonymous Christian Prayer, 3rd-4th century)

….

If Jesus really is the King he claimed to be, and Mary really is the Queen Mother, then it makes sense to ask her to intercede with her Son for us and for a world in need.[8]

The consolidation of the canon of the New Testament took place only in the fourth century and was, in fact, guided by a body of truth that came before it. This body of truth, held by the faithful from the very beginning, included the doctrines and devotions relating to the Mother of Jesus, as even anti-Marians acknowledge.

Mother of Emmanuel

That Mary is Mother of God was evident in Scripture. The apostolic community saw her as such as seen yet again from their devotions and the testimony of the earliest interpreters of Scripture, the Fathers.

The Fathers were unanimous in proclaiming Mary as Mother of God[9]:

Ignatius of Antioch (d. 108)
    "For our God Jesus Christ, according to God's economy, was conceived by Mary of the seed of David (cf. Jn. 7:42; Rom.

3:27), but also by the Holy Spirit." (*To the Ephesians 7, 2*)

Irenaeus (140-202)

"The Virgin Mary, being obedient to his word, received from an angel the glad tidings that she would bear God" (*Against Heresies*, 5:19:1).

Gregory Thaumaturgus (213-270)

"For Luke, in the inspired Gospel narratives, delivers a testimony not to Joseph only, but also to Mary, the Mother of God, and gives this account with reference to the very family and house of David" (*Four Homilies* 1).

Cyril of Jerusalem (315-386)

"The Father bears witness from heaven to his Son. The Holy Spirit bears witness, coming down bodily in the form of a dove. The archangel Gabriel bears witness, bringing the good tidings to Mary. The Virgin Mother of God bears witness" (*Catechetical Lectures* 10:1).

Ephraim (306-373)

"Though still a virgin she carried a child in her womb, and the handmaid and work of his wisdom became the Mother of God" (*Songs of Praise* 1:20).

Athanasius (295-373)

"The Word begotten of the Father from on high, inexpressibly, inexplicably, incomprehensibly, and eternally, is he that is born in time here below of the Virgin Mary, the Mother of God" (*The Incarnation of the Word of God* 8).

Epiphanius of Salamis (310-403)

"Being perfect at the side of the Father and incarnate among us, not in appearance but in truth, he [the Son] reshaped man to perfection in himself from Mary the Mother of God through the Holy Spirit" (*The Man Well-Anchored* 75).

Ambrose of Milan (339-397)

> "The first thing which kindles ardor in learning is the greatness of the teacher. What is greater than the Mother of God? What more glorious than she whom Glory Itself chose?" (*The Virgins* 2:2[7]).

Gregory Nazianzen (329-390)

> "If anyone does not agree that holy Mary is Mother of God, he is at odds with the Godhead" (*Letter to Cledonius the Priest*, 101).

Jerome (342-420)

> "As to how a virgin became the Mother of God, he [Rufinus] has full knowledge; as to how he himself was born, he knows nothing" (Against Rufinus 2:10).
> "Do not marvel at the novelty of the thing, if a Virgin gives birth to God" (*Commentaries on Isaiah* 3:7:15).

Theodore of Mopsuestia (350-428)
"When, therefore, they ask, 'Is Mary mother of man or Mother of God?' we answer, 'Both!' The one by the very nature of what was done and the other by relation" (*The Incarnation* 15)

All-Holy Ark of the Covenant

The Seventh Ecumenical Council, the Second Council of Nicaea, formally addressed Mary by her ancient title *Panagia* meaning "all-holy." Astonishingly this is the feminine form of the Greek word *Panagion* which is the title of the Holy Spirit (see "Panagion and Panagia – The Holy Spirit and the Mother of God" by Paul Evdokimov).

The intimate union between Mary and the Holy Spirit is mapped out in Scripture. Three direct acts of the Holy Spirit in the Gospels involve Mary: the Annunciation when the Spirit "came upon" her, the Visitation when the Holy Spirit "fills" Elizabeth, the Presentation when Simeon "came in the Spirit." Moreover, Mary's prayers help bring about the greatest outpouring of the Spirit in history, Pentecost.

The New Testament verses describing the Holy Spirit's "overshadowing" of Mary are mirror images of the Old Testament portrayal of Yahweh entering the tabernacle. "The Holy Spirit will come upon you and the power of the Most High will cover you with its shadow." (*Luke* 1:35). "The cloud covered the Tent of Meeting and the glory of Yahweh filled the tabernacle." (*Exodus* 40:34).

Two modern Orthodox scholars have extensively explored the ancient understanding of the link between Mary and the Holy Spirit.

> Paul Evdokimov: "The Holy Spirit has no place of incarnation, but he possesses in Mary the unique and altogether distinctive temple of his presence."
> Sergei Bulgakov: "The Holy Spirit is not incarnated in a man but manifests himself in humanity. The Virgin Mary, 'the handmaid of the Lord', is a personality transparent to the action of the Holy Spirit."[10]

In fact, as biblical scholars have shown, other verses concerning Mary in the Gospels of *Luke* and *John* parallel passages about the Ark of the Covenant in the Old Testament. Climactically, in the Book of *Revelation*, the description of the Ark of the Covenant in the Temple in Heaven is immediately followed by the vision of the Woman clothed with the Sun: "The sanctuary of God in heaven opened, and the ark of the covenant could be seen inside it... Now a great sign appeared in heaven: a woman, adorned with the sun." (*Revelation* 11:19-12:1).

Almost instantly, the apostolic community picked up on the connection. Not surprisingly the Blessed Virgin Mary was revered as the Ark of the New Covenant.[11]

Gregory Thaumaturgus (213-270)

> O purest one, O purest virgin, where the Holy Spirit is, there are all things readily ordered. Where divine grace is present the soil that, all untilled, bears bounteous fruit

in the life of the flesh, was in possession of the incorruptible citizenship, and walked as such in all manner of virtues, and lived a life more excellent than man's common standard thou hast put on the vesture of purity has selected thee as the holy one and the wholly fair; and through thy holy, and chaste, and pure, and undefiled womb since of all the race of man thou art by birth the holy one, and the more honourable, and the purer, and the more pious than any other: and thou hast a mind whiter than the snow, and a body made purer than any gold.

Athanasius of Alexandria (295-373)

"O Ark of the covenant surrounded totally and purely on all sides with gold! You are the Ark containing all gold, the receptacle of the true manna, that is human nature wherein the divinity resides." (*De Virginitate*).

"O noble Virgin, truly you are greater than any other greatness. For who is your equal in greatness, O dwelling place of God the Word? To whom among all creatures shall I compare you, O Virgin? You are greater than them all O Covenant, clothed with purity instead of gold! You are the Ark in which is found the golden vessel containing the true manna, that is, the flesh in which divinity resides." (*Homily of the Papyrus of Turin*, 71, 216; Gambero, 106)

"Pure and unstained Virgin." (*On the Incarnation of the Word*, 8; Gambero, 102)

Gregory Nazianzen (329-390)

"He was conceived by the Virgin, who had first been purified by the Spirit in soul and body; for, as it was fitting that childbearing should receive its share of honor, so it was necessary that virginity should receive even greater honor." (Sermon 38, 13; Gambero, 162-163)

Gregory of Nyssa (335-395)

"It was, to divulge by the manner of His Incarnation this

great secret; that purity is the only complete indication of the presence of God and of His coming, and that no one can in reality secure this for himself, unless he has altogether estranged himself from the passions of the flesh. What happened in the stainless Mary when the fulness of the Godhead which was in Christ shone out through her, that happens in every soul that leads by rule the virgin life." (*On Virginity*, 2; NPNF 2, Vol. V, 344)

[T]he power of the Most High, through the Holy Spirit, overshadowed the human nature and was formed therein; that is to say, the portion of flesh was formed in the immaculate Virgin. (*Against Apollinaris*, 6; Gambero, 153)

Cyril of Alexandria (376-444)
"If we look back to the way of the Incarnation of the Only-begotten, we shall see that it is in the temple of the Virgin, as in an ark, that the Word of God took up His abode." (*De Adoratione in Spiritu et Veritate*).

Hail, Mary *Theotokos*, Virgin-Mother, lightbearer, uncorrupt vessel . . . Hail Mary, you are the most precious creature in the whole world; hail, Mary, uncorrupt dove; hail, Mary, inextinguishable lamp; for from you was born the Sun of justice . . . Through you, every faithful soul achieves salvation. (Homily 11 at the Ecumenical Council of Ephesus; Gambero, 243, 245)

Proclus, Patriarch of Constantinople (d. 446), in a homily, applied Psalm 45:5 to her:
"*The Most High has sanctified His own tabernacle. The Incarnate Word dwelled in a womb which He had created free from all that might be to His dishonor.*"

Hesychius of Jerusalem (d. circa 451)
"Arise, Lord, into Your rest, You and the Ark of Your

sanctification, which is very evidently the Virgin Mother of God. For if You are the Pearl, with good reason is she the Ark." (*Sermon V., De S. Maria Deipara*).

Theodotus of Ancyra (early 5th century)
"Hail, O full of grace, the Lord is with you, you are blessed" (Lk 1:28), O most beautiful and most noble among women. The Lord is with you, O all-holy one, glorious and good. The Lord is with you, O worthy of praise, O incomparable, O more than glorious, all splendor, worthy of God, worthy of all blessedness . . . spouse of God, divinely nourished treasure. To you I announce neither a conception in wickedness nor a birth in sin; instead, I bring the joy that puts an end to Eve's sorrow. To you I proclaim neither a trying pregnancy nor a painful delivery . . . Through you, Eve's odious condition is ended; through you, abjection has been destroyed; through you, error is dissolved; through you, sorrow is abolished; through you, condemnation has been erased. Through you, Eve has been redeemed." (*On the Mother of God and the Nativity*; Gambero, 271)

A virgin, innocent, spotless, free of all defect, untouched, unsullied, holy in soul and body, like a lily sprouting among thorns. (Homily VI, 11; O'Carroll, 339)

Modestus, Patriarch of Jerusalem (d. 630)
"It was not an ark made by hands and plated with gold, but a living ark created by God, wholly luminous with the radiance of the all-holy and life-giving Spirit who had visited her."

Sophronius of Jerusalem (560-638)
Others before you have flourished with outstanding holiness. But to none as to you has the fullness of grace been given. None has been endowed with happiness as you, none adorned with holiness like yours, none brought

> to such great magnificence as yours; no one was ever possessed beforehand by purifying grace as were you . . . And this deservedly, for no one came as close to God as you did; no one was enriched with God's gifts as you were; no one shared God's grace as you did. (*In SS Deip. Annunt.* 22; O'Carroll, 329)

Andrew of Crete (650-740)

> Today humanity, in all the radiance of her immaculate nobility, receives its ancient beauty. The shame of sin had darkened the splendour and attraction of human nature; but when the Mother of the Fair One par excellence is born, this nature regains in her person its ancient privileges and is fashioned according to a perfect model truly worthy of God. . . . The reform of our nature begins today and the aged world, subjected to a wholly divine transformation, receives the first fruits of the second creation. (*Homily 1 on Mary's Nativity*; O'Carroll, 180)

> . . . alone wholly without stain . . . (*Canon for the Conception of Anne*; Graef, 152)

John Damascene (675-749)

> O most blessed loins of Joachim from which came forth a spotless seed! O glorious womb of Anne in which a most holy offspring grew. (*Homily I on the Nativity of Mary*; O'Carroll, 200; cf. Graef, 154; Gambero, 402)

The Akathistos hymn called Mary "Ark of the Holy Spirit's gilding!"

The Latin and Syriac Fathers joined the Greek Fathers in proclaiming Mary's freedom from sin. The Syrian St. Ephrem of Edessa, for instance, said, "There is in you, Lord, no stain, nor any spot in your mother."

The liturgies of the early Church echo the faith of the apostolic community:

The Coptic liturgy of St. Basil
Most of all, the pure, full of glory, ever virgin, the holy Mother of God, Saint Mary; who in truth, gave birth to God the Word.[12]

The Byzantine liturgy of St. John Chrysosthom
Priest – Especially for our most holy, pure, blessed, and glorious Lady, the Theotokos and ever-virgin Mary.
People: It is truly right to bless you, Theotokos, ever blessed, most pure, and Mother of our God. More honorable than the Cherubim, and beyond compare more glorious than the Seraphim, without corruption you gave birth to God the Logos. We magnify you, the true Theotokos.[13]

Mother of the Faithful

We see in *Revelation* 12:17 that the dragon "went off to wage war against the rest of her offspring, those who keep God's commandments and bear witness to Jesus."

The idea that Mary was the Mother of all the faithful was taken for granted by the early Christians. This is apparent in the catacomb images and devotions of the apostolic community (see the next section). It is apparent also in the writings of the early Fathers[14]:

Irenaeus (140-202)
"The Word will become flesh, and the Son of God the son of man—the Pure One opening purely that pure womb, which generates men unto God." (*Against Heresies*, 4, 33, 12)

Epiphanius of Salamis (310– 403)
"The whole race of man upon earth was born of Eve; but in reality, it is from Mary that Life was truly born to the world, so that by giving birth to the Living One, Mary might also

become the Mother of all the living. (*Against Eighty Heresies*, 78, 9).

Basil the Great **(329-379)**

"O sinner, be not discouraged, but have recourse to Mary in all you necessities. Call her to your assistance, for such is the divine Will that she should help in every kind of necessity."

Ambrose of Milan (339-397)

"Eve is called mother of the human race, but Mary Mother of salvation." (*Epistle 63*, No. 33).

Jerome (347-419):

"Even while living in the world, the heart of Mary was so filled with motherly tenderness and compassion for men that no-one ever suffered so much for their own pains, as Mary suffered for the pains of her children."

Augustine (354-430):

"The Mother of the Head, in bearing Him corporally became spiritually the Mother of all members of this Divine Head." (*Of Holy Virginity* 6).

Intercessor

The faithful saw Mary as an intercessor on their behalf and, as at Cana, sought her assistance in their needs.

Ephrem the Syrian (306-373)

O Immaculate and wholly-pure Virgin Mary, Mother of God, Queen of the world, hope of those who are in despair: You are the joy of the saints; you are the peacemaker between sinners and God; you are the advocate of the abandoned, the secure haven of those who are on the sea of the world; you are the consolation of the world, the ransom of slaves, the comfortress of the afflicted....

O great Queen, we take refuge in your protection. After God, you are all my hope. We bear the name of your servants; allow not the enemy to drag us to hell. I salute you, O great mediatress of peace between men and God, Mother of Jesus our Lord, who is the love of all men and of God, to whom be honor and benediction with the Father and the Holy Ghost. Amen. [15]

Blessed Virgin, immaculate and pure, you are the sinless Mother of your Son, who is the mighty Lord of the universe. Since you are holy and inviolate, the hope of the hopeless and sinful, I sing your praises. I praise you as full of every grace, for you bore the God-Man. I venerate you; I invoke you and implore your aid. Holy and Immaculate Virgin, help me in every need that presses upon me and free me from all the temptations of the devil. Be my intercessor and advocate at the hour of death and judgment. Deliver me from the fire that is not extinguished and from the outer darkness. Make me worthy of the glory of your Son. O dearest and most kind Virgin Mother. You indeed are my most secure and only hope, for you are holy in the sight of God, to whom be honor and glory, majesty and power forever. Amen.

Athanasius of Alexandria (295-373)
"It is becoming for you, O Mary, to be mindful of us, as you stand near Him who bestowed upon you all graces, for you are the Mother of God and our Queen. Come to our aid for the sake of the King, the Lord God and Master Who was born of you. For this reason you are called "full of grace.""

Be mindful of us, most holy Virgin, and bestow on us gifts from the riches of your graces, O Virgin, full of grace.[16]

John Chrysostom (349-407)
"Hail, O Mother! Virgin, heaven, throne, glory of our Church, its foundation and ornament. Earnestly pray for

us to Jesus, your Son and Our Lord, that through your intercession we may have mercy on the day of judgment. Pray that we may receive all those good things which are reserved for those who love God. Through the grace and favor of Our Lord, Jesus Christ, to Whom, with the Father and the Holy Spirit, be power, honor, and glory, now and forever. Amen."[17]

Augustine (354-430)

"Blessed Virgin Mary, who can worthily repay you with praise and thanksgiving for rescuing a fallen world by your generous consent? What songs of praise can our weak human nature offer in your honor, since it was through you that it has found the way to salvation?

Accept then such poor thanks as we have to offer, unequal though they be to your merits. Receive our gratitude and obtain by your prayers the forgiveness of our sins. Take our prayers into the sanctuary of heaven and enable them to make our peace with God. May the sins we repentantly bring before Almighty God through you be forgiven. May what we beg with confidence be granted through you. Accept our offering and grant our request; obtain pardon for what we fear, for you are the sole hope of sinners. We hope to obtain the pardon of our sins through you. Blessed Lady, in you is our hope of reward. Holy Mary, help those who are miserable, strengthen those who are discouraged, comfort those who are sorrowful, pray for your people, plead for the clergy, intercede for all women consecrated to God. May all who venerate you experience your assistance and protection.

Be ready to aid us when we pray, and bring back to us the answers to our prayers. Make it your continual concern to pray for the People of God, for you were blessed by God and were made worthy to bear the Redeemer of the world, who lives and reigns forever."[18]

Virgin Mary

The apostolic community spoke of the Mother of Jesus as the Virgin Mary. As seen here[19] and elsewhere, they saw her as "ever-virgin." This will be discussed further in the next section.

Ignatius of Antioch (d.108)

"The virginity of Mary, her giving birth, and also the death of the Lord, were hidden from the prince of this world: three mysteries loudly proclaimed, but wrought in the silence of God." (*Letter to the Ephesians* 19:1)

Justin Martyr (100-165)

"He became man by the Virgin."

Irenaeus (140-202)

"What the virgin Eve had bound in unbelief, the Virgin Mary loosed through faith."

(*Against   Heresies   3:22:4*)

[Isaiah] says, "Behold, the Virgin shall conceive and bear a Son, and He, being God, is going to be with us" (Isa. 7:14). And whilst, as it were, astonished at this thing, he makes known what will come about, that God will be with us. And concerning His birth, the same prophet says in another place, "Before she who was in labour gave birth, and before the birth pains came on, she was delivered of a male [child]" (Isa. 66:7); [thus] he indicated the unexpected and extraordinary birth from the Virgin. (*The Demonstration of the Apostolic Preaching,* 54)

Hippolytus of Rome (179-235)

"For whereas the Word of God was without flesh, He took upon Himself the holy flesh by the holy Virgin." (*Treatise on Christ and Antichrist,* 4)

Clement of Alexandria (150-215)

"When the loving and benevolent Father had rained down the Word, that Word then became the spiritual nourishment of those who have good sense. O mystic wonder! The Father of all is indeed one, one also is the universal Word, and the Holy Spirit is one and the same everywhere; and one is the Virgin Mother. I love to call her the Church. This Mother alone was without milk, because she alone did not become a wife. She is at once both Virgin and Mother: as a Virgin, undefiled; as a Mother full of love." (*The Instructor of the Children,* 1:6:42:1)

3 WHAT ALL FIRST MILLENNIUM CHRISTIANS AFFIRMED

Theotokos (Mother of God), Panagia (All-Holy), Heavenly Intercessor, Aeiparthenos (Ever-Virgin)

Mary – What All First Millennium Christians Affirmed

Role	Council	Liturgies
Theotokos (Mother of God)	✔	✔
Panagia (All-Holy)	✔	✔
Heavenly Intercessor	✔	✔
Aeiparthenos (Ever-Virgin)	✔	✔

The apostolic proclamation pertaining to Mary that permeated both Scripture and the life of the early Christians was unanimous, universal and unequivocal.

It was taken for granted as true at the same level as teachings on the Incarnation and the Trinity. By all. It was firmly held across the Christian world from Rome, Gaul and Spain to Central Asia and Africa (North Africa, Egypt and Ethiopia) – all the ancient hubs of Christianity. And it promulgated without hesitation the truth that the Mother of Jesus is Mother of God, all holy, perpetually virgin, assumed into Heaven and interceding for us who are her children.

How do we know all this? From the devotional practices of the earliest Christian communities still preserved in extant documents, from the ancient liturgical families of all the churches founded by the Apostles and evangelists – Rome (Peter and Paul), Alexandria (Mark, disciple of Peter), Antioch (Peter), Jerusalem (James), Persia (disciples of Thomas), Constantinople (Andrew) – from the writings of the "Fathers" both East and West and from the definitive teachings of the first Councils and creeds of the undivided Church.

Much as the original apostolic proclamation pertaining to Jesus and the Trinity had to be clarified and refined by the early Church Councils, so too the teachings on Mary had to be systematically distilled by the same Councils. But the primordial proclamation itself – as evidenced by scriptural texts, liturgical formulas and devotional practices – preceded the organically continuous and universally binding definitions of the Councils. This proclamation was an inextricable part of the entirety of Scripture, liturgy, devotion and conciliar teaching that has always been known as Christianity. Pick and choose was never an option!

In fact, if we were to reject one element of this ancient body of teaching – such as the doctrines relating to Mary – then consistency demands that we also reject the other elements such as the doctrines of the Trinity or the two natures and one Person in Christ. These latter doctrines are not taught in so many words by Scripture but the people who were closest to the human authors of Scripture understood these authors to be teaching certain doctrines about the Triune God, the incarnate Son of God and the Virgin Mary. These doctrines stand or fall together: picking and choosing was neither logically nor historically defensible.

To be sure, there were individual dissenters from the apostolic proclamation. But the dissenters almost always came in later centuries and rejected what had always been accepted as integral to Christianity by the community as a whole. The early Councils were called both to clarify and re-affirm what was already believed and to refute speculations that contradicted the apostolic body of teaching.

Collectively, the teachings of the earliest Councils, the texts of the ancient liturgies, the writings of the first and later Fathers and the devotions of the faithful show us a historic Christian consensus about Mary, the Mother of Jesus, present at the very beginning that extended over the first one thousand five hundred years of Christendom. It was a consensus that both the apostolic community and the New Testament reveal a Mary who was the Immaculate (Council of Constantinople III), All-holy (Nicaea II), Perpetually Virgin (Constantinople III) Mother of God (Ephesus, Chalcedon), Mother of Humanity and Intercessor before the Trinity (Nicaea II).

This consensus stayed faithful to the proclamation of the apostolic community.

We have reviewed the scriptural accounts and the apostolic proclamation relating to the Mother of Jesus. We will now consider the pillars underpinning the subsequent Christian consensus: the ancient devotions, the liturgies, the writings of the Fathers and the teachings of the Councils. Following that we will delve into the details of five specific teachings: Mary's divine maternity, her holiness and freedom from sin, her assumption into Heaven, her intercession and her perpetual virginity.

Devotions

The catacombs of the Christian martyrs of the second and third centuries not only show images representing the scriptural stories but also images of the Virgin in which her mediation is invoked for protection and defense. "The earliest surviving Christian art is preserved on the walls of tombs belonging to wealthy Christians in the catacombs of Rome. … Possibly the earliest known image of the Virgin Mary independent of the Magi episode, is a fresco dated about 150 CE in the Catacomb of Priscilla on the Via Salaria in Rome that shows her nursing the infant Jesus on her lap."[1]

On the significance of the images in the catacombs, John F. Murphy writes, "We might say that devotion to Mary was born in the catacombs. In the catacombs Mary is depicted in both historical and symbolical representation. In the latter, when she is more than part of a scriptural scene, she is portrayed both with and without the Divine Child. … The number of representations of Mary and especially the locations where they are found indicate that she was not considered a mere historical personage."[2]

We get some idea of what the early Christians thought about the Virgin Mary from prayers like the famous *Sub Tuum Praesidium*, found in an Egyptian papyrus from approximately 250 A.D., that formed part of the Coptic Christmas liturgy: "We fly to thy patronage, O holy Mother of God; despise not our petitions in our necessities, but deliver us always from all dangers, O glorious and blessed Virgin. Amen."

Another interesting, though startling, resource pool is the set of second century apocryphal gospels and third century *Transitus Mariae* narratives. Now these were obviously fantasies with no basis in historical fact but, nevertheless, they do show us something important. The idea that the Blessed Virgin was the most important participant in salvation history after her Son was so rooted in the minds and hearts of the faithful that some of them felt compelled to invent stories about Jesus and Mary that paid homage to their exalted status. What is important here is not the story but the state of mind that led to the invention of the story: these stories were written by and for people who already took the adoration of the Lord and the veneration of the Virgin for granted.

Liturgies

Perhaps the truest witness to the faith of the believing community is the language of their prayer and liturgical celebration. All of the ancient liturgies (Greek, Syriac and Latin), even those before the Council of Ephesus, testify to the firm belief of the Christian faithful in the veneration of Mary and the invocation of her intercession.

The Eastern liturgies, the most ancient of them all since Christianity sprang in the East, resonate with hymns, odes and prayers to the Virgin Mary.

Hundreds of hymns in the Byzantine liturgy are written in honor of Mary: "While we sing the glories of thy Son, we praise thee, too, O Mother of God, living Temple of the Godhead. O purest One, do not despise the petitions of the sinner." "Hail, Mother of God, Virgin full of grace, Refuge and Protection of the human race."

The Alexandrian liturgy is also replete with Marian veneration and invocation: "Hail to thee, O Virgin, the very and true Queen; hail glory of our race." "Hail Mary! We beseech thee, holy one, full of glory, ever Mother of God, Mother of Christ, lift up our prayers to thy beloved Son, that He may forgive us our sins."

The Antiochene liturgy used all across Syria and Palestine, perhaps the oldest of the ancient liturgies, includes the liturgy of St. James. The Marian invocations in this latter liturgy, such as the following recited during the breaking of the Host, "My blessed Lady Mary, beseech with thine only Begotten that he be appeased through thy prayers and perform mercy on us all," are profoundly moving.

In the Western liturgies, Marian veneration and invocation appears in the liturgy of the Mass and also forms a prominent part of regular prayers (offices) and feasts.

These liturgies celebrate all of the privileges of Mary ranging from her Divine Maternity to her Virginity, Sanctity, Assumption and Mediation.

The Fathers

The Church Fathers were the great, ancient teachers of Scripture. Any doctrine taught unanimously by the Fathers of East and West was regarded as normative by that very fact. These are the same holy thinkers whose teachings and interpretations helped guide the Councils to their conclusions. The writings of all of the Church Fathers, the Teachers of the earliest Christian communities who interpreted Scripture for the faithful, bear eloquent testimony to Marian veneration. In their scripturally derived understanding of Mary as the New Eve and the Ark of Covenant, Mother of God and Mother of Christians (cited in the previous section) the Fathers established an unassailable basis for Marian veneration that was accepted for centuries by the Christians of East and West.

Councils

The first seven Ecumenical Councils of the undivided Church proclaim the convictions held in common by all Christians for the first sixteen centuries about the role of Mary in salvation history. No Christian can reject these Councils since to reject them would *ipso facto* mean rejecting the teachings of the Councils about such articles of faith as the Holy Trinity. The Trinity is not a word used in the Bible but it is an interpretation of certain biblical passages ratified by the Councils of the Church. To believe in the Trinity is implicitly to accept the authority of the Councils that taught the doctrine of the Trinity. If one accepts the doctrine of the Trinity then one has also to accept the Marian doctrines taught by the Councils – since both doctrines are ultimately accepted on the authority of the bodies that taught them.

"*Theotokos*," "Mother of God," as mentioned earlier, was the first formally defined title of Mary. It was declared as definitive Christian doctrine at the Council of Ephesus in 431 A.D.: "We confess the holy virgin to be the *mother of God* because God the Word took flesh and became man and from his very conception united to himself the temple he took from her."

The Council of Ephesus gave a new doctrinal momentum to the great wave of Marian veneration and invocation that had been building up in previous centuries. After this Council, more churches were named after her, new prayers were addressed to her, and great feasts in her honor were introduced into the Church's calendar.

The Second Council of Constantinople (553 A.D.) condemns those who denied the doctrine of Mary's Divine Maternity: "If anyone ... does not formally confess that she is properly and truly the mother of God, because he who before all ages was born of the Father, God the Word, has been made into human flesh in these latter days and has been born to her ... let him be *anathema*."

The language of the seven Ecumenical Councils, accepted as

authoritative by Protestants, Catholics and Orthodox alike, gives some idea of the reverence that Christians had for their Mother.

The Fifth Ecumenical Council (Second Council of Constantinople, 553) describes her as "the holy, glorious and ever-Virgin Mary."

"The Virgin Mary" was "really and truly the Mother of God," says the Third Council of Constantinople (680).

Finally, and most significantly, the Seventh Ecumenical Council (the Second Council of Nicaea, 787) proclaims, "The Lord, the apostles and the prophets have taught us that we must venerate in the first place the Holy Mother of God, who is above all the heavenly powers. If any one does not confess that the holy, ever virgin Mary, really and truly the Mother of God, is higher than all creatures visible and invisible, and does not implore with a sincere faith, her intercession, given her powerful access to our God born of her, let him be anathema."

The Seventh Ecumenical Council taught that veneration of the Virgin extends to veneration of her images for, as the Council taught, "[We] define with all certitude and accuracy that just as the figure of the precious and life-giving Cross, so also the venerable and holy images, as well in painting and mosaic as of other fit materials, should be set forth in the holy churches of God, and on the sacred vessels and on the vestments and on hangings and in pictures both in houses and by the wayside, to wit, the figure of our Lord God and Saviour Jesus Christ, of our spotless Lady, the Mother of God, of the honourable Angels, of all Saints and of all pious people. ... For the honour which is paid to the image passes on to that which the image represents, and he who reveres the image reveres in it the subject represented."

The Old Testament condemns idolatry, the worship of graven images and the attribution of deity to any man-made object, but the very book that condemns such idolatry also has Yahweh commanding the construction of images of angels (as do other books of the Bible). Martin Luther's interpretation of Old Testament passages on idolatry is helpful, "Nothing else can be drawn from the words: 'Thou shalt have no strange gods before me' except what relates to idolatry. But where pictures or sculptures are made without idolatry, the making of such things is not forbidden." Luther also said, "If I have a painted picture on the wall and I look upon it without idolatry, that is not forbidden to me and should not be taken away from me."[3]

Mary is *Theotokos*, Mother of God the Son, *Panagia*, the All-Holy who is Spouse of God the Holy Spirit, and *Aeiparthenos*, Ever-Virgin. All three truths were defined by Ecumenical Councils of the undivided Church. As noted, the Seventh Ecumenical Council formally addressed Mary by her ancient title *Panagia* meaning "all-holy" which is the feminine form of the Greek word *Panagion* that is the title of the Holy Spirit.

The authoritative Councils of the Church and the ancient liturgies testify to the truth of Mary's holy and immaculate state. Mary is called "the holy Virgin" by the Council of Ephesus (431) and as "the holy, glorious and ever-Virgin Mary" by the Second Council of Constantinople (553). The Third Council of Constantinople (680) describes her as "our Lady, the holy, immaculate, ever-virgin and glorious Mary, truly and properly the Mother of God." Even more significant, the Third Council of Constantinople studied the Synodal Epistle of Sophronius and declared that it is "in accordance with the true faith and with the Apostolic teachings, and with those of the holy approved Fathers." In his Epistle, Sophronius stated that Mary is "holy, immaculate in soul and body, entirely free from every contagion."

In the five appendices below, we will consider in more detail various misconceptions about the truths relating to Mary. What does it mean to say she is Mother of God? What precedents are there for saying that she is All-Holy? Why do we say she was assumed into

Heaven? Do we worship Mary? How can we claim that she was always a virgin when the Gospels speak of the brothers and sisters of Jesus?

Appendix 1

Mother of God?

Quite obviously, to say Mary is the Mother of God is not to say that she is Mother of the infinite Mind and Will that is God or that she brought an infinite divine Person into being. Rather, what is being said is that God the Son took his human nature from her. Mary is the mother of Jesus who is a divine Person with a divine nature and a human nature. She is not the mother of a "nature" which would be unintelligible but of a divine Person *in his human nature*. She did not "create" the divine Person but this pre-existent Person took his human body wholly from her (his human soul, of course, coming from God).

To deny this teaching is to say that there is both a divine person and a human person in Christ. He is made up of two persons! But such a view contradicts what we see in the Gospel narratives. Jesus has two natures, divine and human, but he is one Person, albeit a divine Person. In the Gospels, we see him acting primarily through the human nature he has acquired from Mary although, as a divine Person, he also has a divine nature.

Despite being the Mother of God, Mary is entirely human. In fact, it is precisely because she is a human person that her Son receives his human nature from her. But the kind of relationship she has with the Son of God makes her unique in the history of humankind and of all creation. Eric Mascall explains:

> If he [Jesus] had only been a very holy person with whom God had formed a very close association, then presumably Mary would have been related to him in the same way that any other mother is related to her son and nothing more. There would have been nothing particularly unique about this. The important thing, the coming of God to dwell

in Jesus, would have happened *after* she had fulfilled her function. But when it was fully realized and claimed that the Son of God, God the Son, took his human nature from her, then it was seen that she had an absolutely unique function above all other mothers and above all other human beings. There is not, never has been and never will be anybody else from whom God has taken human nature in order to live in it himself. There is only one Incarnation, and therefore there is only one Mother of the Incarnate."

Human history and particularly the history of the People of Israel, he says, were divinely guided precisely to "produce" the Mother of God:

When it is seen that that [to be the Mother of God] is her [theological] function, then one can see that the whole history of the Jewish people, and indeed the whole history of the human race, is focused on her, because it was the purpose of God that he should take human flesh and become a member of the human race in order to redeem it. Because of that, the whole of human history is concentrated on this moment. Of course, to the ordinary secular historian, it may not look exactly like that. There are certain things that have happened in human history that do not seem to have any connection with this. But when one is asking what the meaning of human history is, when one asks why it was that God chose the Jewish race to be his people, and why he did the things with it which he did, the answer is that it was in order to produce a woman who could be the mother of God, one from whom God could take human flesh. The Incarnation is not like a flash of lightning suddenly coming out of a completely blue sky; it is not something for which there were no apparent causes or antecedents. God did not work that way. No doubt he might have done so, but he did not. In fact he prepared the setting for the Incarnation: it was in the *fullness of time*, as the Apostle tells us, that God sent forth his Son born of a woman, born under the Law, to redeem those who were born under the Law. And therefore the whole purpose in the mind of God, from the moment in which he called Israel to be his people, was that in Israel there should be a woman from whom God the Son could take human nature and who could become his mother. …

If one asks what was God's purpose when he formed Israel, the answer is that it was the production of the Mother of God. He himself became man as a Jew, he became man as the son of a Jewish mother.[4]

Because her Son took his human nature from her, says Mascall, the relation between Mary and the divine Trinity is entirely unique:

If what took place in the Incarnation was not just the bringing into existence of another human being but the actual taking of human nature by the pre-existent Son of God, if the Word *became flesh*, then the relation between Mary and her Son was radically different from the relation which any other human mother has to her son and indeed the relation between Mary and the Holy Trinity was radically different from the relation which any other human being has to God.[5]

Gerald Van Ackeren notes that her Motherhood is a mirror image of the eternal Father's Fatherhood:

Because Mary has generated the Son of God, she now possesses the human perfection of motherhood in a manner which makes her the most perfect possible created image of the Eternal Father. She is like the Father in being by way of generation to His divine Son. Only the Eternal Father and Mary have generated the same eternal Person, He according to His divine nature, she according to His human nature.[6]

<u>Appendix 2</u>

All-Holy?

In addition to the testimony of Scripture and the apostolic community, the insight that Mary is immaculately conceived, free of sin, is compelling for a number of other reasons.

It has precedents in Old and New Testaments where we see that individuals who have been chosen by God for an important mission have been purified by him beforehand. Thus, sanctity was conferred on both Jeremiah and John the Baptist while they were still in the womb.

The Protestant scholar Charles Augustus Briggs, a professor at Union Theological Seminary in the early 20th century, offered the scriptural and theological rationale for the truth of Mary's immaculate conception:

> Though Jesus partook of flesh and blood, we were not obliged to think that he partook of any hereditary sin or corruption. When now we consider, not only that Jesus became flesh, but that he was born into this world, of a human mother, we have all the more to consider how he could have been conceived and born without sharing, with all others of human kind, in original sin and and hereditary inclinations to sin. …

> May we not suppose that the Holy Spirit had been sanctifying the holy line for generations, preparing it for that fulness of the time when the Messiah was to be born of it, and that in Mary the Mother of our Lord that sanctifying had reached the supreme point of entire removal from her, even at her birth, of all the taint and defilement of original sin, so that she was fitted from her birth by purity, innocence, and consecrated sanctity to be the Mother of our Lord. …

> The holy Mother, pure and undefiled, immaculate and altogether sacred, had been prepared through many generations of holy ancestry, as the consummate flower of humanity, to bear as her fruit the holy child.[7]

Of course, Mary's immaculate conception does not in any way mitigate her need for the Savior. But whereas all other Christians were delivered from their sins by their baptism into Christ, Mary was preserved from sin. The redemptive effects of Christ's death were applied to her at conception because these effects could go backward and forward in time.

Such preservation was required because the Savior could not be born of a person who was under the slavery of sin, and therefore of Satan, for even an instant. Moreover, she could not be the New Eve if she was herself one of the fallen.

Appendix 3

Assumed into Heaven?

The ancient, authoritative and universal proclamation of Mary as the New Eve entailed certain inexorable corollaries. To be truly the partner of the New Adam, she could not be under the reign of sin and Satan. Hence the teaching of her life-long holiness and freedom from sin which, we have seen, is specifically affirmed in Scripture. Further, since she was preserved from Original Sin, she could not suffer its consequences which includes bodily corruption ("you are dust, and to dust you shall return"). Here again Scripture confirms the inescapable truth that the New Eve was taken body and soul into Heaven as the first beneficiary of the New Adam's victory. How else can we interpret the famous Scriptural revelation of the Mother of the Messiah appearing in her heavenly glory (which presupposed her already being in Heaven)?

> "A great sign appeared in the sky, a woman clothed with the sun, with the moon under her feet, and on her head

> a crown of twelve stars. … She gave birth to a son, a male child, destined to rule all the nations with an iron rod. Her child was caught up to God and his throne." (*Revelation* 12: 1,5).

We have seen why that, taken as it stands, there can be little doubt that the Woman Clothed with the Sun is the Virgin Mary.

But the teaching of Mary's assumption into Heaven faced a major challenge.

The Book of *Revelation* was not considered divinely inspired until the fourth century, so its unmistakable reference to Mary's physical presence in Heaven was not available to the earliest Church Fathers as an authoritative reference point. Nevertheless, the appearance of the Woman Clothed with the Sun makes it clear that the assumption of Mary into Heaven was evident from apostolic days. The doctrinal formulation of this event was inevitably delayed by the fact that *Revelation* itself was included in the canon only later. Eusebius of Caesarea (d. 339) and other historians left *Revelation* out of their listings of the New Testament books. It was only included in the canon authorized by the fifth and sixth century Popes.

The delay in the inclusion of *Revelation* in the canon, among other reasons, slowed down official recognition of the Assumption of Mary. Nevertheless, there were three other powerful testimonies to the truth of the Assumption.

The first is negative in nature. There is no place on earth which is revered as the final resting place of the body of the Virgin Mary. Yes, there are tombs where she is supposed to have been buried prior to the Assumption – but none which is said to currently contain her body. Moreover, there are no relics of her body available to the faithful. This is remarkable because the graves of the Apostles and the saints have been pilgrimage destinations for centuries. And relics of the saints have always been in high demand. So the fact that there is no claim made about the remains of the Queen of the Apostles and the Saints is startling – startling unless indeed it was common knowledge that her body had been assumed into Heaven.

Secondly, there is the earlier mentioned body of literature known as the *Transitus Mariae* made up of apocryphal narratives of the Assumption of Mary. There are Greek, Latin, Syriac, Coptic and other versions of these accounts indicating that they were common across the Christian world of the time. According to Stephen Shoemaker, in his *Ancient Traditions of the Virgin Mary's Dormition and Assumption*, these writings originated in the third century at the latest. They are works of fiction with no historical value. Nevertheless, they are important in bearing witness to the early Christian conviction that the body of the Blessed Virgin was taken up into Heaven.

The third testimony is more significant because it concerns the inclusion of the Assumption in the liturgy. From at least the fourth century, August 15 was celebrated as the Feast of the Dormition, the death and Assumption of the Virgin. The Byzantine Emperor officially decreed its celebration in the East by the end of the sixth century and Pope Sergius promulgated it in the West in the seventh century.

Francis Davis recounts the history, "It will help us in our theological account of the doctrine to see how Christians eventually became fully and explicitly conscious of it. First of all it became reflected in the Liturgy. There was already a feast in the fifth century called the "Memory of the Mother of God," observed on differing days around Christmas in some Eastern countries, and on 15 August in others. Many think this feast was first observed in Ephesus after the Great Council. It was certainly connected with the devotion to the ever-Virgin *theotokos*. Once the nature and dignity of the Son were fully established in Ephesus and Chalcedon, the full dignity of the Mother began also to be appreciated. … It was this early feast which developed into the feast of Our Lady's passage to heaven."[8]

There is also a tradition that the Assumption was disclosed at the Council of Chalcedon. The account is found in the *Euthymiac History* which is quoted in the *Synaxarion of Constantinople* and other writings: "St. Juvenal, Bishop of Jerusalem, at the Council of Chalcedon (451 AD), made known to the Emperor Marcian and Pulcheria, who wished to possess the body of the Mother of God, that Mary died in the presence of all the Apostles, but that her tomb, when opened upon the request of St. Thomas, was found empty; wherefrom the Apostles concluded that the body was taken up to heaven."[9]

The scriptural and theological argument for the Assumption was well presented by Bernard Lonergan, described in *Time* magazine as "the finest philosophic thinker of the 20th century":

> Mary's position is a position of privilege: full of grace, she never for an instant was under the dominion of Satan or stained by sin; ever a virgin, still she was a mother, the mother of God, and she became a mother without the pangs of motherhood, for those pangs were the curse of Eve (Genesis 3:16) and she was blessed among women (Luke 1:42) to be called blessed by all generations (ibid, 48). Who but she could be the woman spoken of in Genesis: "I will put enmities between theeand the woman, and thy seed and herseed: she shall crush thy head, and thous shalt like in wait for her heel" (Genesis 3:15). But can all this be granted, and yet the assumption be denied?Can we say tthat the fruits of the redemption were anticipated to preserve the soul of Mary from original sin but not anctipated to bring her body to heaven? Can one say she was freed from the empire of Satan, inasmuch as that empire was sin, but inasmuch as that empire was death? Can one say that she adores in heaven the body to which she gave birth yet is without the body that gave it birth? Can one invent some metaphysical law or some principle of divine justice that overrules the best of sons' love for the best of mothers, that permits the Sacred Heart to be a living heart but forces the Immaculate

Heart to be a dead heart, that calls a halt to privilege after the immaculate conception, divine maternity and perpetual virginity, to consign our Lady's body to the grave? Can one deny that the assumption would be a grace, or that Mary is full of grace? The more one thinks about it, the more numerous the aspects one considers, the fuller becomes the evidence and the greater its cogency."[10]

<u>Appendix 4</u>

Do Those Who Seek Her Intercession Worship Mary?

One of the most common misconceptions about the Christian approach to Mary is the idea that any attempt to seek her intercession is tantamount to worship.

Nothing could be further from the truth. And the rejection of intercession is contradicted by our daily experience.

All things in the world are mediated through different agents. This is especially true in the history of salvation which is a story of mediators from Abraham, Isaac and Jacob to Moses, David and the Prophets, from the One Mediator ("one" in the sense of "primary") Jesus Christ to the Joseph, Mary, the Apostles and all Christians. We receive faith through the mediation of friends and family, through the Bible, a document that mediates words and ideas.

The idea that God is the only agent on the platform of history is simply false to everyday and historic Christian experience. We are not puppets but mediators of the message of salvation. As Paul put it, we are "co-workers with God;" and, "in my flesh I am filling up what is lacking in the afflictions of Christ on behalf of his body, which is the church." (*Colossians* 1:24). Mediation is a fundamental reality of our daily experience and of our life as a Christian. Only pantheists would say that God is the only agent. The revelation of God in Christ, on the contrary, calls us all to be agents. We grow closer to God as we exercise our freedom in his service.

Some Christians frown on belief in the intercession of the saints claiming that it is unbiblical or incompatible with faith in God's total sovereignty. Such disdain would have been incomprehensible to the early Christians (even the catacombs have prayers to the blessed dead). It also flies in the face of the biblical narratives. The Book of *Revelation* is a classic instance of the saints in Heaven intervening in earthly affairs. The questions of mediation and the intercession of those in Heaven are treated in more detail in the last section.

Here we want to clarify that worship in the sense of adoration or the offering of sacrifice can only be directed to God. No finite person should be worshipped and to do so would be both idolatrous and blasphemous.

Only the Triune God should be worshipped. But God is glorified when we marvel at his creation or admire his works. Mary is a creation of God who is "our tainted nature's solitary boast" in Wordsworth's words. Scripture says that she is to be blessed by all generations. To do so is to venerate her. This is not worship. As Elizabeth said, Mary is to be "blessed" because she "believed." Moreover, Mary was given to us by God as our Mother to help us our earthly journey.

Of course, there is no comparison in the order of nature or the supernatural order between Jesus and Mary. Jesus was a divine Person, Mary was through and through human. But the second Person of the Trinity took on a human nature and worked with and through human beings to bring the effects of his redemptive death to the human race. You can choose to be one of his instruments or you can refuse. Mary was the first to say Yes. And as *Revelation* 12:17 points out, she is the mother of all who profess Jesus.

To thank her for saying "Yes," to follow her example of living a holy life, to seek her help as our divinely-provided mother is not "worshipping" her. Rather, it is to do what is biblically mandated. It is to accept and cherish this tender loving gift given to us by our heavenly Father.

Christians of the apostolic community would not feel at home in a present-day community that has no place for the Mother of Jesus as our Mother and intercessor.

<u>Appendix 5</u>

Perpetual Virginity?

Among the Marian truths affirmed by Councils, liturgies and the faithful is the perpetual virginity of the Blessed Virgin. Not only was the birth of Jesus a Virgin Birth in that he had no biological father but his Mother remained a virgin after he was born. Jesus did not have biological siblings. This truth was affirmed by all Christians including the architects of the Protestant Reformation who took pains to show that no biblical passage was inconsistent with it. Martin Luther, in fact, called Mary's Perpetual Virginity an "article of faith." The roots of the doctrine were too deep, well-grounded and organically embedded for it to be denied or disputed. But like other ancient teachings, the Perpetual Virginity of the Virgin Mother was discarded by both "liberal" and Fundamentalist Christians starting in the 19th century. Yet the truth of this affirmation is apparent to those who consider it in the light of both Scripture and the entirety of Christian doctrine.

On the face of it, the Gospel references to Jesus' brothers and sisters may seem to contradict the historic doctrine. But, even on the face of it, there is no doubt from the texts that some of those called "brothers" are not actually siblings of Jesus which means that we cannot simply stay "on the face of it." Brant Pitre observes, "The first and most important reason for concluding that the 'brothers' of Jesus are not children of Mary is also the most often overlooked.

It is this: The Gospels themselves explicitly state that the so-called brothers of Jesus are in fact the children of another woman named Mary. In order to see this clearly, all we need to do is compare the identities of the 'brothers' of Jesus in the account of Jesus' ministry in Nazareth with the accounts of the people present at his crucifixion and burial. … On the one hand the Gospel of Mark indisputably identifies 'James' and 'Joses' as two of the brothers (Greek *adelphoi*) of Jesus (Mark 6:3). … On the other hand – and this is crucial – the Gospel of Mark also provides solid evidence that the same two men, *'James' and 'Joses' are the sons of a different woman named Mary*."[11]

In the normal course of things, when reading a text we should adopt the simplest and most obvious interpretation of its content. The burden of proof is on anyone who wishes to argue to the contrary. But when two sets of texts in the same work say something seemingly contradictory then it behooves us to take a more nuanced approach. The burden of proof, in fact, is on those who ignore the conflict and defiantly insist on sticking with their preferred version.

With this preview, we turn to ten truths that testify to the perpetual virginity of Mary of Nazareth. The ten fall under three categories: framework of interpretation, textual evidence and theological considerations.

Framework of Interpretation

1 Councils and Doctrines

Every doctrine is an interpretation. Now the Bible is not simply a novel concerning which different literary critics can foist their own creative spins. Christians consider it to be an account of God's revelation to humanity. Nevertheless, it is a revelation laid out in specific written narratives and letters. How should these narratives and letters be understood? Where are the boundaries between "historical episode" and "theological teaching"? What about the nuances of translation? When there is an obvious theological statement ("Faith without works is dead") how is it to be understood?

As we have seen, there are two basic approaches to this problem: either there is one authoritative interpretation of the divine Word that holds true from the inception of the Church to the present day or every believer determines the interpretation of all biblical passages on his or her own. Protestants, like Catholics and Orthodox, for the most part, hold that there are certain interpretations of biblical passages that are normative and binding for all believers, thus implicitly acknowledging the role of authoritative interpretations.

Those authoritative interpretations that we have today did not simply spring out of some individual's claim to testimony from the Holy Spirit. In point of fact, two key sources of these authoritative interpretations are the witness of the Church Fathers and the teaching of the first seven Ecumenical Councils. In practice, Protestants like Catholics and Orthodox take the interpretations of the Councils to be definitive. Some Protestants may not put as much stock in the Fathers but they do accept the dogmatic definitions of the Councils.

Now some might say they accept the Councils because the conciliar teachings conform with Scripture. But it can then be asked how they know that the Councils' teachings conform with Scripture. If they say that in their personal opinion the Councils are faithful to Scripture then the ultimate arbiter is personal opinion. But if the Trinity has no greater basis for its truth than personal opinion then you cannot fault someone whose personal opinion leads them to reject the doctrine as "unbiblical." Pushed into this corner, most of them concede that the Councils do have some level of authority in determining the interpretation of Scripture when it comes to key doctrines.   The few who have no role for the Councils end up in one of two places: either they leave Christianity as a whole because no one can really decide what is Christian doctrine or (inconsistently) they stick to the teachings of the Councils while saying the Councils have no authority. As a whole, however, most Protestant denominations accept the teachings of the Councils.

Now it so happens that three of the Seven Ecumenical Councils of the undivided Church affirmed Mary's perpetual virginity in the clearest terms. As we have seen, the Second Council of Constantinople (553) spoke of "the holy, glorious, ever-Virgin Mary." The Third Council of Constantinople (680) accepted and ratified the teaching of the First Lateran Council (649) which decreed, "If anyone does not in accord with the Holy Fathers acknowledge the holy and ever virgin and immaculate Mary was really and truly the Mother of God, inasmuch as she, in the fullness of time, and without seed, conceived by the Holy Spirit, God in the Word Himself, who before all time was born of God the Father, and without loss of integrity brought Him forth, and after His birth preserved her virginity inviolate, let him be condemned." The Seventh Ecumenical Council (the Second Council of Nicaea, 787) spoke of "the holy, ever virgin Mary."

Faced with this clear teaching, Catholics, Orthodox and Protestants up to the 19th century accepted the perpetual virginity of Mary as a truth of faith and a binding interpretation of the scriptural texts. Today, many deny the doctrine without realizing its roots in the Councils of the Church. But if they deny one dogma defined by one of these Seven Ecumenical Councils, then in terms of their own frame of reference, they cannot consistently affirm any of the other dogmas as authoritative. You cannot consistently say that the Council was authoritative in some interpretations but not in others (how could you know which is authoritative and which is not?). You cannot have your cake and eat it too. It is all or nothing. The doctrine of Mary's perpetual virginity is a defined dogma of the Seven Ecumenical Councils along with other foundational doctrines of Christianity. If you reject the Councils' authority, when it comes to this doctrine. then you cannot consistently defend any of its other doctrines as authoritative. So, a denial of Mary's perpetual virginity strikes at the very root of orthodox Christianity.

2 The Consensus of the Faithful

Next, under the category of interpretation is the witness of the Fathers of the Church. It is a striking fact that no Father of the

Church, East or West, has denied the perpetual virginity of Mary. Several have written their own striking expositions of the doctrine. Jose Pedrozo notes that Fathers with different styles and agendas taught the doctrine: Athanasius of Alexandria, Ephrem of Syria, Hilary of Poitiers, John Chrysostom, Ambrose of Milan, and Augustine of Hippo. Of one Father, Tertullian, it has been said that he seemed to be in doubt about the doctrine – but Pedrozo has shown that Tertullian's comments were ambiguous at best.[12] Now the Fathers were closer in time to the apostolic era. They were closer to the writers of Scripture and their intentions and to the beliefs of the first Christians than anyone today. And yet these great witnesses speak with one voice about the fact that Mary was always virgin. Why should we discount their interpretations? And this is precisely why no Christian seriously questioned the doctrine for 19 centuries (with one solitary exception: Helvidius, Jovinian and Bonosus dissented from the doctrine in the last two decades of the fourth century but this dissent died a quick death after it was roundly condemned by the Fathers).

The consensus on the matter did not change with the Protestant Reformation as we shall see. Luther, Calvin and Zwingli firmly held to the continuing virginity of Mary.

Now it seems unthinkable – and therefore unbelievable – that a doctrine held as definitive Christian truth by all Christians for nearly 2000 years can be rejected as false simply because a few Christians in the 20th and 21st centuries decided that all previous generations of Christians were wrong. After all, no new facts have turned up, no new textual passages have been discovered. What has happened is simply that certain iconoclasts have decided that they will cut themselves free of their roots and strike out on their own. Why should we trust these iconoclasts whose own interpretations are subjective, arbitrary and liable to change in a generation or less? Not surprisingly, those Christians who retain belief in the Virgin Birth while denying Mary's perpetual virginity will eventually end up losing belief in both.

This was the prescient warning issued by the Reformer Ulrich Zwingli: "It was not enough that the conception of Jesus take place without a male role, for if a woman who had previously known a man had conceived him even through the Holy Spirit, 'who would ever have believed that the child that was born was of the Holy Spirit? For nature knows no birth that is not besmirched with stain.' For the same reason she had to be ever a virign, she who bore the one in whom there could not be even the least suspicion of blemish. For the birth of Jesus to be absolutely pure of every stain, Mary herself had to be free of any pollution of normal child-bearing."[13] Historically this was what happened. The Enlightenment rejection of the doctrine of perpetual virginity accompanied the denial not simply of the Virgin Birth but of the divinity of Christ.

3 The Witness of the Liturgy

The third hard fact is the liturgy. Perhaps the truest witness to the faith of the believing community is the language of their prayer and liturgical celebration. All of the ancient liturgies, even those before the Council of Ephesus, testify to the firm belief of the Christian faithful in the veneration of the "ever-Virgin." The Byzantine liturgy for instance proclaims, "O Christ, behold Thy Mother, she who conceived Thee in her womb, without the loss of her virginity, and who after she had given Thee birth remained a stainless Virgin." The Ethiopian liturgy declares, "O holy praiseful ever-virgin Parent of God, Mother of Christ." These are the great prayers that formed the Christian soul, the database that transmits to this very day the living faith of the Apostles.

The decline of a full-blooded faith in modern times can be traced at least partially to the loss of the ancient liturgy in its fullness. Christians who do not live the liturgy of their fathers in faith are like fish out of water and so cannot hope to recognize the true teachings of ancient Christianity. The loss of the liturgy results, first, in the loss of a living faith and the sense of the sacred and, second, in the loss of the doctrines that constitute Christianity.

The Textual Evidence

From all of the above, it is clear that the Christian framework of interpretation cannot countenance anything less than the perpetual virginity of the Mother of Jesus. So how does this view stack up against what we read in the New Testament texts? It is here that the critics triumphantly claim victory pointing to those passages that speak of Jesus' brothers and sisters. And at first blush it might seem that the critics have an open and shut case. Take the main passages:

> "While he was still speaking to the crowds, his mother and his brothers appeared outside." (*Matthew* 12:46)
> "Is not his mother named Mary and his brothers James, Joseph, Simon, and Judas? Are not his sisters all with us?" (*Matthew* 13:55)
> "Isn't this the carpenter, the son of Mary, a brother of James and Joses and Judas and Simon? Aren't his sisters our neighbors here?" (*Mark* 6:3).
> "His mother and brothers arrived." (*Mark* 3:31).
> "Then his mother and his brothers came to him." (*Luke* 8:19).
> "After this, he and his mother, [his] brothers, and his disciples went down to Capernaum." (*John* 2:12).
> "So his brothers said, 'Leave here and go to Judea….'For his brothers did not believe in him." (*John* 7:3ff).
> "All these devoted themselves with one accord to prayer, together with some women, and Mary the mother of Jesus, and his brothers." (*Acts* 1:13).
> "Do we not have the right to take along a Christian wife, as do the rest of the apostles, and the brothers of the Lord." (I *Corinthians* 9:5).
> "But I did not see any of the other apostles, only James the brother of the Lord." (*Galatians* 1:19).

But things are not quite as simple as the critic would like them to be. Which brings us to the first textual truth.

Children of Mary?

Nowhere does Scripture speak of the children of Mary. It does speak of Mary, mother of Jesus, but never of Mary, mother of Jesus, James, Joses, Simeon, Jude and various daughters. Moreover, it can be argued that Scripture in fact specifies that Mary had only one son. "Is he not the carpenter, the son of Mary?," we read in Mark 6:30. Notice here that we are talking of "the" son of Mary not "a". It has been pointed out that this is a scriptural usage applied to the only son of a widow (hence no mention of Joseph).

The Smiths and the Joneses
But this is just the beginning. In point of fact, we have what seems to be an open and shut case that at least two of the four so-called brothers of Jesus were sons of a different mother. In the Gospel accounts of the crucifixion we are given a glimpse of the women who stood under the cross: "Among them were Mary Magdalene and Mary the mother of James and Joseph, and the mother of the sons of Zebedee. … But Mary Magdalene and the other Mary remained sitting there." (*Matthew* 27:56, 61). "There were also women looking on from a distance. Among them were Mary Magdalene, Mary the mother of the younger James and of Joses, and Salome. … Mary Magdalene and Mary the mother of Joses watched where he was laid. When the Sabbath was over, Mary Magdalene, Mary the mother of James, and Salome bought spices." (*Mark* 15:40,47; 16:1). In *Matthew* 13 we read of James and Joseph, the brothers of Jesus. In *Matthew* 27 we read that this James and Joseph are the sons of "the other Mary". In *Mark* 6 we read of James and Joses, the brothers of Jesus. In *Mark* 15-16, the same James and Joses are seen to be the sons of another Mary. Whatever else we might say and speculate, it is a hard fact then that James and Joses/Joseph who were called brothers of Jesus were not in fact his blood brothers.

Harold Riley points out that Matthew never introduces names without identification.[14] Thus, the brothers of Jesus, "James and Joseph" of *Matthew* 13, are used to identify the Mary who is their mother in *Matthew* 27. Riley notes that Mark is less meticulous in his introductions than Matthew but even he refers the James and Joses of *Mark* 6 to their mother in *Mark* 15, 16. The pattern is present in *Luke* although it is less direct. Given the unity of authorship of the Gospel of *Luke* and the *Acts of the Apostles*, Riley observes that Luke simply introduces the "other" Mary as "the mother of James" (*Luke* 24:10) in his Gospel because his reader will know all about James from *Acts*.

What about Judas and Simon, the other "brothers," and the "sisters" of Jesus? The Bible does not have much to say on this beyond the cryptic opening of the epistle of *Jude*: "Jude, a slave of Jesus Christ and brother of James." (*Jude* 1:1). We shall see, however, what the earliest historians of the Church had to say about the matter. But before that we should note that in Matthew 27 and Mark 15 James and Joses/Joseph are mentioned before Simon and Judas. We know that the first two were not Jesus' blood brothers and it seems most unlikely that Simon and Judas would be mentioned after them if they were indeed blood brothers. The same goes for the "sisters."

One source of confusion is the bewildering array of Jameses and Marys in the New Testament.

Let's start with the Jameses. There is James the Greater, son of Zebedee and the brother of the Apostle John. Then there is James the Lesser, the Son of Alphaeus. Then we have James the brother of Joseph/Joses who is the son of "the other Mary." Finally we have James the brother of the Lord, bishop of Jerusalem, who is also called an Apostle. We could add to the mix James the brother of the author of the epistle of *Jude*.

With regard to the Marys, we have Mary the mother of Jesus, Mary Magdalene, Mary the mother of James and Joses and Mary of Clopas. "Standing by the cross of Jesus were his mother, and his mother's sister, Mary the wife of Clopas, and Mary Magdalene" (*John* 19:25).

So who's who here? One possible approach is this. James the Lesser is described in the Gospels as "James, the son of Alphaeus." (*Matthew* 10:3). "Clopas," it has been pointed out, is the Greek form of the Aramaic name "Alphaeus." Mary of Clopas is then the mother of James and Joseph/Joses and the James in question here is also the Apostle James the Lesser. Clopas, according to the earliest Church historians, was the brother of Joseph and therefore his sons would be cousins of Jesus – or "brothers" in Aramaic usage. Thus, James is called one of the brothers of Jesus in the Gospels and then "the brother of the Lord" in the *Acts of the Apostles* and in *Galatians*. One item from early tradition is relevant here. It has been held that after the death of Joseph, Jesus and Mary lived with the family of Clopas (possibly in Capernaum). This would make Clopas' children foster-brothers and sisters of Jesus – and hence the reference to them as brothers and sisters of Jesus was more natural even than "cousins".

The life of James the Just, bishop of Jerusalem, has been recorded both by the Jewish historian Josephus and the second-century Christian writer Hegesippus. Hegesippus also sheds light on Simon/Simeon, the brother of the Lord mentioned in the Gospels: "After James the Just was martyred, on the same charge as the Lord, then Simeon being also his [Jesus'] uncle's child, the son of Clopas, was appointed as bishop, as second in succession, being put forward by all, being the cousin of the Lord."[15] Hegesippus pointedly says about Judas that he was "called his [the Lord's] brother;"[16] here "called" implies that he was not actually a blood brother. Thus there is good reason to believe that James, Joseph, Simon, Judas and their sisters were children of Clopas and Mary.

Further studies into the kinfolk of Jesus would be fascinating given their special place both in biblical times and the life of the early Church.

Implications of the Virgin Birth

Like the Catholics and Orthodox, traditional Protestants too are committed to belief in the virginal conception of Jesus – an event unveiled in the Gospels of *Matthew* and *Luke*. Now if indeed

Jesus was born of a Virgin, then his "brothers and sisters" could not possibly be brothers and sisters in the full physical sense. If Protestant Fundamentalists were right and Mary did have other children, at best they would be Jesus' half-brothers and half-sisters. This being the case, Protestants too will have to admit that "brother" and "sister" are not being used in the normal sense. They too have to go beyond the literal text to "interpret" it in terms of a theological framework.

7 Oh Brother!
Which brings us to the question of "adelphos." Scholars have shown that Hebrew and ancient Aramaic did not have different words for "brother", "cousin", "uncle" and "kinsman". One and the same word was used to describe all these different relationships ("ah"). The Greek translation of the Old Testament reflects this pattern of usage. To take one well-known example, Abraham's nephew Lot is called his brother in Genesis. Although Greek does have different words for "brother," "sister," "cousin" and "kinsman", i.e., "adelphos," "adelphe", "anepsios" and "sungenis," the authors of the Greek Old Testament (as no one disputes) continued their Hebraic/Aramaic habits of thought and used just a single term for cousins, brothers, half-brothers, nephews and kinfolk. "Adelphos" was used with the primary meaning of kinfolk and secondary meanings of brother, cousin and the like; for sisters and kinswomen the word used was "adelphe" (siblings and kinsfolk collectively were "adelphoi"). This seems clearly to be the case in the New Testament as well which is written in the same style of Greek as the Old and uses Greek words with Hebrew ones in mind ("Semitisms"). How else can we explain the fact that James and Joseph are called brothers of Jesus when they have a different mother – let alone the fact that the virginally conceived Jesus is said to have brothers and sisters? The "cousins" argument is by no means a desperate ploy introduced to save a dying argument. It is, in fact, the only plausible explanation for the entire range of data, the only solution that can keep up with the Joneses and the Smiths. (To be sure, "anepsios" is used one time but this is in an epistle with 33 other words not found anywhere else in

the New Testament; a possible reason for this is explained below.)

The theologian François Rossier considers the issue of terminology:
There are no "cousins" in the New Testament, except for one case. We find the word *anepsios* once, in Colossians 4:10. Most scholars today think that the Letter to the Colossians was not written by Paul, but probably by a disciple of his from the second generation of Christians with a Greek background. Otherwise, we find the word *adelphos* 343 times in the New Testament (and *adelphê*, "sister," 26 times), but no other "cousin." The only family relationship that existed among people of a same generation in the New Testament seems to be brotherhood. Is it relevant, since we know that in Judaic society the inmost family group was not limited to the nuclear family as we know it in North America or in Europe? Other Greek words such as *homopatôr* ("half-brother by the father") or *homomêtôr* ("half-brother by the mother") are also not found in the New Testament. If the authors of the New Testament wanted to render the relationships within Jesus' family as precisely as possible in Greek, they should have used such expressions since--and Matthew and Luke make it very clear--Jesus was not the true son of Joseph. If Jesus' "brothers" were sons of Mary, they would have been only Jesus' "half-brothers by the mother," and there was a Greek word for that. ...
Nowhere in the New Testament are the "brothers" of Jesus also identified as "sons of Mary" within the same context. Whereas, again in Mark 6:3, Jesus is identified as "the son of Mary" by the people of Nazareth. ...

The vast majority of the Fathers of the Church, supporting either the Epiphanian or the Jeromian hypothesis, belonged to the Greek culture and spoke Greek. Some of them were even close to the New Testament era in both time and culture. Yet they did not find it an obstacle to consider Jesus' *adelphoi* as his cousins, step-brothers or half-brothers. The tradition adopted that point of view--be it the Catholic one, the Orthodox one, or even the Reformation one (with Luther and Calvin)--until the nineteenth century, when Protestant biblical scholars started to question the consensus in the name of the historical-critical method of interpretation. Their views were widely adopted within the Protestant denominations, making of Mary's perpetual virginity one of the great markers of dissent.[17]

Terms and their meanings continue to be relevant.   For instance, there is no Thai word for "tourist". They do have a word for "guest" which is deployed to include tourists as well. More to the point, to this day in certain ethnic groups (e.g., in countries like India) cousins call themselves brother and sister.

8 Miscellaneous

Another relevant fact is Mary's question to the Angel Gabriel: "How can this be since I have no relations with a man" (*Luke* 1:35). She, of course, knew that she was betrothed to Joseph as well as how procreation takes place. But this intriguing reply has been plausibly interpreted as a signal that Mary had made a commitment of virginity even within marriage. "Mary certainly would not have spoken those words if she had not vowed her virginity to God," wrote Augustine.

Brant Pitre remarks that. "Once we realize that Mary is already legally married, the first part of her question to Gabriel – 'How shall this be …?' – appears to make no sense. In the words of the atheist scholar Gerd Ludemann: 'Mary's question is hard to reconcile with v. 27: a fiancée can hardly be surprised at the promise of a child even if she has as yet had no sexual intercourse with her fiancée.' Along similar lines, the famous Protestant scholar Rudolf Bultmann once admitted that 'Mary's question' is an 'absurd one for a bride.' … Just as someone who says 'I do not smoke' means 'I do not smoke (presently), nor do I have any intentions of smoking (in the future),' so Mary's words mean, 'I do not have sexual relations (presently), nor do I intend to have relations (in the future).'"[18]

Moreover, if Joseph and Mary had other children they were certainly not born before Jesus who was the first-born. From the biblical record it is clear that for the first 12 years of the life of Jesus, there were no siblings on the horizon.

Two objections to Mary's perpetual virginity hinge on certain verses.

"He [Joseph] had no relations with her until she bore a son, and he named him Jesus." (*Matthew* 1:25). Does this mean, as the critics say, that Joseph had sexual relations after Jesus was born? No, it is a negative statement that he was not involved in the conception of Jesus not a positive statement that he had relations after the birth of Jesus. In his notes to the Geneva Bible (1560), John Calvin points out that "Neither yet doest this worde (til) import always a time following: wherein the contrarie may be affirmed, as our Saviour, saying that he wil be present with his disciples, til the end of the world meaneth not, that after this worlde he wil not be with them." A manual of Methodist doctrine said about this verse: "It cannot be inferred from that expression, 'Michal had no child till the day of her death' (2 Sam 6:23) that she had children afterward."[19]

Another line of attack centers on *Luke* 2:7: "And she gave birth to her firstborn son." Here it should be noted that according to the Jews the child that opened the womb is the first-born (*Exodus* 13:2; *Numbers* 3:12). There is no implication that the child is the first of many. An ancient tomb inscription states that the mother died as she was giving birth to her first-born. As John Calvin put it, "first-born" refers to the fact "she had never none before, and not in respect of any she had after."

9 Faithful Son
A decisive confirmation of Mary's perpetual virginity case appears at the very end of the life of Jesus when he entrusts his mother to

the care of the Apostle John. Now, if he had siblings, this would be unthinkable not simply in the Semitic society of the day but many other societies as well. According to Jewish law, the oldest son (the first-born) has the responsibility of looking after his parents. This could be passed on only to his brothers (if he had any). So seriously did Jesus take this responsibility that his final act before quenching his thirst and giving up his spirit was the care of his mother. And he fulfills his duty by placing her under the care of a friend whom he trusted and loved. If he had any immediate siblings, such a transfer would not have been permissible or required. In fact it would have been deeply insulting. It would have been especially galling to James, the brother of the Lord and first bishop of Jerusalem, if Mary had indeed been his mother. But the fact that Jesus entrusted his mother's care to John shows clearly that he, and only he, was the Son of Mary.

Theological Considerations

10 Spouse of the Spirit
There is yet another dimension to this question that is often ignored and this is a theological truth about Mary proclaimed by the ancient Church. Remember: the Seventh Ecumenical Council formally addressed Mary and the Holy Spirit by the same name (*Panagia* and *Panagion*).
Given these ancient biblical insights into Mary's spousal union with the Holy Spirit, her virginal motherhood of the Word incarnate and her spiritual maternity of all Christians, the notion that she was not ever-Virgin was both incongruent and repugnant. The biblical basis for this was already laid in Old Testament times. When God told Moses to prepare the Israelites for his coming, he said, "'Go to the people and have them sanctify themselves today and tomorrow.' … Then Moses came down from the mountain to the people and had them sanctify themselves and wash their garments. He warned them, … 'Have no intercourse with any woman.'" (*Exodus* 19:10,14-5). This was the condition set forth simply to see a manifestation of the divine power. In the case of Mary, there was a union unique

in all human history between a human person and God. Moreover, according to Jewish tradition, the prophets all became celibate after the Word of the Lord was communicated to them.

From this review of the ten truths, we see why the Christian community from the very beginning has consistently affirmed the perpetual virginity of Mary. We have seen also that a comprehensive study of both the biblical texts and historical accounts of the early Church substantiates the idea that the brothers and sisters of Jesus were not the children of Mary. Finally, we have the theological *tour de force* crafted by the Fathers and the Councils from the biblical texts: Mary is the Spouse of the Holy Spirit and the spiritual mother of all Christians.

Jointly and severally, the ten truths constitute a compelling case for the belief that Mary was indeed "ever-virgin."

#4 WHAT THE PROTESTANT REFORMERS AND MODERN PROTESTANT THINKERS PROFESSED

*All-Holy Virgin Mary, Mother of God,
Mother of Believers*

What the Protestant Reformers and Modern Protestant Thinkers Professed

Teaching About Mary	Luther	Calvin	Zwingli
Mother of God	✓	✓	✓
All-Holy	✓		✓
Virgin	✓	✓	✓
Assumed into Heaven	✓		✓
To be honored	✓	✓	✓

The fourth data-set in our inquiry may come as a surprise to anti-Marian Protestant Fundamentalist and Evangelical Christians. It is this: The leading lights of the Protestant Reformation affirmed almost all the teachings about Mary proclaimed by the apostolic community. In fact, the first major proponent of *sola scriptura*, Martin Luther, saw nothing unbiblical about the affirmation that Mary, the Mother of Jesus, is Mother of God, All-Holy, Ever-Virgin and assumed into Heaven and should be venerated. What is more, prominent Protestant thinkers of the last few decades – Lutherans, Anglicans/Episcopalians, Presbyterians, Methodists, Baptists and others – have powerfully expounded these and other important truths relating to Mary.

These trends have been highlighted in many major media stories.

But first let us consider the writings on Mary of the progenitors of the Protestant Reformation.

Martin Luther

"She is rightly called not only the mother of the man, but also the Mother of God ... It is certain that Mary is the Mother of the real and true God."[1]

"It is an article of faith that Mary is Mother of the Lord and still a Virgin."[2]

"But the other conception, namely the infusion of the soul, it is piously and suitably believed, was without any sin, so that while the soul was being infused, she would at the same time be cleansed from original sin and adorned with the gifts of God to receive the holy soul thus infused. And thus, in the very moment in which she began to live, she was without all sin."[3]

"She is full of grace, proclaimed to be entirely without sin – something exceedingly great. For God's grace fills her with everything good and makes her devoid of all evil."[4]

"There can be no doubt that the Virgin Mary is in heaven. How it happened we do not know."[5]

"The veneration of Mary is inscribed in the very depths of the human heart."[6]

"Is Christ only to be adored? Or is the holy Mother of God rather not to be honoured? This is the woman who crushed the Serpent's head. Hear us. For your Son denies you nothing."[7]

John Calvin

"Elizabeth called Mary Mother of the Lord, because the unity of the person in the two natures of Christ was such that she could have said that the mortal man engendered in the womb of Mary was at the same time the eternal God."[8]

"Helvidius has shown himself too ignorant, in saying that Mary had several sons, because mention is made in some passages of the brothers of Christ."[9]

We should receive the Word of God "According to the example of the holy Virgin, that each one should conform to the respect she showed for the Word of God."[10]

About Mary's question to the boy Jesus in the Temple: "She was not pushed by any pride, but this query was prompted by three days of sorrow."[11]

"It cannot be denied that God in choosing and destining Mary to be the Mother of his Son, granted her the highest honor."[12]

"To this day we cannot enjoy the blessing brought to us in Christ without thinking at the same time of that which God gave as adornment and honour to Mary, in willing her to be the mother of his only-begotten Son."[13]

Ulrich Zwingli

"It was given to her what belongs to no creature, that in the flesh she should bring forth the Son of God."[14]

"I firmly believe that Mary, according to the words of the gospel as a pure Virgin brought forth for us the Son of God and in childbirth and after childbirth forever remained a pure, intact Virgin."[15]

"I esteem immensely the Mother of God, the ever chaste, immaculate Virgin Mary."[16]

"Christ ... was born of a most undefiled Virgin."[17]

"It was fitting that such a holy Son should have a holy Mother."[18]

"The more the honor and love of Christ increases among men, so much the esteem and honor given to Mary should grow."[19]

To be sure, these leading lights of the Protestant Reformation rejected Marian mediation and intercession given their doctrines of *sola gratia* and *sola fidei*. This is a topic we will study in the next section. But they saw nothing unscriptural in the historic teachings relating to the person of Mary. This is acknowledged even in an Evangelical critique of Marian teachings: "Most remarkable to modern Protestants is the Reformers' almost universal acceptance of Mary's continuing virginity, and their widespread reluctance to declare Mary as a sinner."[20]

In "The Blessed Virgin Mary in the Protestant Tradition", Methodist church historian David Butler writes,

> In the period before the Reformation there were few who offered protests against Mary or Marian devotion. One of the amazing facts of history is that there are very few disrespectful references to Mary either before or after the Reformation. Perhaps four reasons might be offered for this:
>
> ɪ.   The evidence of he Council of Ephesus in AD 431 which defined Mary as the *Theotokos* or Mother of God said something important christologically which could not be combatted without making nonsense of the Incarnation.
>
> ɪɪ.   Mary is seen in the writings of many authors as the exemplar of faith, the one who said her *fiat mihi* to God at the Annunciation. As an example of faith, she could only be held in reverence, not criticised for the extravagant devotion offered to her by some believers. After all, justification by *faith* became the doctrinal yardstick of the Protestant Reformation.
>
> ɪɪɪ.   The pre-eminence of Christmas as a festival over even Easter as a major Christian festival means that Mary still holds the centre stage with her Son at least once a year even within the Protestant tradition.
>
> ɪⱳ.   The use of the Magnificat of Mary in the services of the Book of Common Prayer in the Anglican tradition. This kept the thought of Mary as the one who saw God overturn the presuppositions of humanity in her life of faith.[21]

But the ancient veneration of the Virgin has been lost in modern times. Did this loss come about from a re-discovery of what the Bible teaches? The answer is "No" since the faithful in ancient times were familiar not just with the New Testament narratives but, sometimes, with the authors of these narratives. Moreover, if the Christian community had been wrong for all these centuries in its fundamental beliefs about the Woman whose "Yes" resulted in the Incarnation, then there is no reason to believe it was right on any other doctrine. The doctrines and devotions relating to the Virgin Mary, we have seen, are inextricably intertwined with Christianity as a whole.

The historic consensus began to fragment in the seventeenth through the nineteenth centuries under the influence of the Enlightenment. A good many of the heirs of the Reformation rejected not simply Marian doctrine but ever larger chunks of the patrimony of faith be it doctrines about Christ and the Trinity or acceptance of the divine inspiration of the Bible.

Partially in reaction to this erosion of faith, the twentieth century saw the emergence of the Fundamentalist, Evangelical and Pentecostal movements within Protestant Christianity. In one way or another, these movements sought to reclaim the heritage of the Reformers. In this process, sadly, they rejected key elements of the historic consensus about Mary that had been embraced by the Reformers.

Marian doctrines and devotions were now dismissed as unscriptural innovations, refined paganism and works-centric, Christ-obscuring superstitions. In rejecting Marian doctrines, some of the Fundamentalists fell into ancient heresies ranging from Arianism and Adoptionism to Nestorianism and Monophysitism. It is in this context that the present-day Protestant recovery of the ancient teachings about Mary is so important. It is important because it represents also a return to the historic Christian consensus. Given that there are today over 45,000 Protestant denominations, each with their own different views of the Christian message, it would seem that the idea of *sola scriptura* has morphed into a scriptural free-for-all. Consequently, a deeper understanding of the ancient consensus may serve as a centripetal impulse that counteracts the centrifugal forces fragmenting Christendom.

Prominent theologians from mainstream Protestant denominations now accept historic Marian titles like Mother of God while giving qualified assent to various Marian doctrines (for instance, the Immaculate Conception). These include theologians from the Anglican/Episcopalian, Presbyterian, Lutheran and Methodist denominations.

Some Evangelical Protestant theologians now admit that Protestants have failed to notice, let alone honor, the Virgin Mary and should rectify this oversight. They are quick to add that any attention to Mary must be tempered by the content of Scripture.

These trends were highlighted in a *Time* magazine cover story titled, "Hail, Mary: Catholics have long revered her, but now Protestants are finding their own reasons to celebrate the mother of Jesus" (March 21, 2005), an *Economist* article called "A Mary for All" (December 18, 2003), and cover stories in various Protestant publications ranging from the Evangelical *Christianity Today* ("The Blessed Evangelical Mary") ("The First Christian") to the liberal *Christian Century* ("St Mary for Protestants").

Below are excerpts from some of these stories:

"Hail Mary", Time, March 21, 2005
>In a shift whose ideological breadth is unusual in the fragmented Protestant world, a long-standing wall around Mary appears to be eroding. It is not that Protestants are converting to Catholicism's dramatic exaltation: the singing of Salve Regina, the Rosary's Marian Mysteries, the entreaty to her in the Hail Mary to "pray for us sinners now and at the hour of our death." Rather, a growing number of Christian

thinkers who are neither Catholic nor Eastern Orthodox (another branch of faith to which Mary is central) have concluded that their various traditions have shortchanged her in the very arena in which Protestantism most prides itself: the careful and full reading of Scripture.

Arguments on the Virgin's behalf have appeared in a flurry of scholarly essays and popular articles, on the covers of the usually conservative *Christianity Today* (headline: The Blessed Evangelical Mary) and the usually liberal *Christian Century* (St. Mary for Protestants). They are being preached, if not yet in many churches then in a denominational cross section--and not just at modest addresses … but also from mighty pulpits like that at Chicago's Fourth Presbyterian Church, where longtime senior pastor John Buchanan recently delivered a major message on the Virgin ending with the words "Hail Mary … Blessed are you among us all."

This could probably not have happened at some other time. Robert Jenson, author of the respected text Systematic Theology, chuckles when asked whether the pastor of his Lutheran youth would have approved of his (fairly extreme) position that Protestants, like Catholics, should pray for Mary's intercession. … A growing interest, on both the Protestant right and left, in practices and texts from Christianity's first 1,500 years has led to immersion in the habitual Marianism of the early and medieval church. …

[Princeton Scripture specialist] Beverly Gaventa … approached her Mary work in "a Protestant sort of way. We pride ourselves on reading Scripture, so let's read Scripture and see what we find."

What she read--and what Protestants had been more or less skimming for centuries--was a skein of appearances longer and more strategically placed than those of any other character in the Gospels except Jesus. …

Gaventa's conclusion was that although Mary's appearances can be brief and frustratingly devoid of anecdote, "there isn't a figure comparable to her." No major player appears earlier in the story, and none, she notes, "is present in all these key situations: at Jesus' birth, at his death, in the upper room." Protestant treatments, Gaventa asserted, tended to limit themselves to what God does through Mary rather than talk about Mary herself.

"Protestants and Marian Devotion – What about Mary?", Jason Byassee, Christian Century, December 14, 2004

Much of what being Protestant has historically meant has involved a protest against the Catholic devotion to Mary. … But recently there has been a flurry of publications by Protestants on Mary, works that suggest she could be an ecumenical bridge -- or at least that the Protestant aversion to Marian devotion is eroding. …

Church historians of all stripes have long granted that Marian teaching and devotion dates from the earliest days of the church. And they grant that devotion to Mary was not discarded even by the leading Reformation figures Luther, Calvin and Zwingli. …

The most important contribution of these recent reflections is to give fresh attention to the incarnation. …

What she lacks in quantity of appearance in scripture she makes up for in quality. Luke's telling of the gospel begins with her, and her *fiat* ("let it be' in Latin) to Gabriel's announcement of God's incarnational intent opens the way for a new eruption of grace into the world. She is present at and indeed an instigator of Jesus' first miracle at Cana in Galilee (John 2: 1-11). She and other women are present at the cross, when the male disciples flee. Depending on how one reads the resurrection narratives, she is present there too (Mark 15:40; 47).

It is striking that Mary is in the upper room at Pentecost -- the only woman present there who is named -- to receive the outpouring of God's Spirit at the birth of the church (Acts 1:14). When Paul makes his one oblique mention of Jesus' mother it is to point to her as a sign that he was indeed born, and so was genuinely human (Gal. 4:4). To cite a more contested passage, her image in Revelation 12:17 as a woman clothed with the sun with a crown of stars in the agony of giving birth to a son who will rule the nations is, at the very least, impressive. Mary's appearances in scripture are indeed limited, but they are tied to crucial moments in salvation history, without which there would be no church.

Scripture presents Mary as an important agent in her own right, not just as the mother of her son. If her Magnificat is any indication, she is an extraordinary reader of the Bible, lyrically weaving together Jewish scripture into a new song that is perhaps the most frequently sung canticle in church history. We are twice told that she "treasures" the words entrusted to her by angels and shepherds and that she "ponders these things" in her heart (Luke 2:19, 51). Aged Simeon promises her that her child's destiny to be for the "falling and rising of many in Israel" will cause a "sword to pierce" her own soul too -- suggesting that Mary's importance continues in the saga of salvation long after her child's birth. (Luke 2:34-35). …

Her womb was the physical site of the enfleshment of God. This leads Robert Jenson to a conclusion that may sting Protestant sensibilities -- we ought to ask Mary to pray for us.

Jenson argues that death does not sever the bonds of the body of Christ -- as even most Protestant eucharistic prayers make clear. To ask for a departed saint's prayer, then, is not in principle different from asking another Christian for her prayers. We hold that the saints are not simply gone but are ever alive to God, and so we ought also consider them to be available as intercessors, and powerful ones at that.

This is precisely the point at which Protestant theologians get most nervous. Such a request of prayer from Mary smacks of an effort to gain divine favor by some route other than Christ -- the height of idolatry. To prop the door open here even an inch threatens to bring back the medieval system of veneration of scores of saints in an effort to earn the favor of a distant and foreboding Jesus. Hence we slam the door shut. To honor Christ, the saints must be excluded.

Yet this needn't be so. Jenson insists that "the saints are not our way to Christ; he is our way to them." Each saint's particular graces can be seen as reflections of the grace of Christ, whose greatness grows in our eyes as we attend to the saints' individual stories. The strengthening of the bonds of the body of Christ, stretching as they do across the divide between earthly life and death, should bring tribute to Christ rather than discredit.

"The Blessed Evangelical Mary," *Timothy George, Christianity Today, December 5, 2003*

Honoring Mary certainly doesn't come naturally to Protestants. For complex historical reasons, to be a Protestant has meant not to be a Roman Catholic. To worship Jesus means not to honor Mary, even if such honor is biblically grounded and theologically sound. But, as the Reformers were quick to point out, Mary is the embodiment of grace alone and faith alone, and thus contemporary Protestants, along with the Reformers, should highly extol Mary in our theology and worship.

"The First Christian," Christianity Today, November 22, 2019
> Mary's preeminent example as a Christ follower neither began nor ended at Christmas.

Once upon a time, the Virgin Mary pervaded the life and thought of the Western world. Her presence was so expansive, in fact, that even European fairy tales acknowledged her status. Take Cinderella. An abusive stepmother was still the cause of Cinderella's impoverished conditions, but in one of the earliest tellings of the tale, she knew the one to call upon was the Virgin Mary. In no time at all, Cinderella's hunger was resolved, and a prince was proposing. By replacing the Virgin Mary with a Fairy Godmother, the story of Cinderella was successfully secularized for today without disenchanting it. But it's not just fairy tales that have stripped Mary from a well-loved story. She's missing from The Story, too.

It's not that Protestants have entirely forgotten Mary. At this time of year, the mother of Jesus gets some attention. But Mary is not a Christmas figure to be stored away like the manger and the Star of Bethlehem until next year. She played an extraordinary role throughout the life and ministry of Jesus, from the Annunciation to the day of Pentecost. By overlooking the roles she played throughout Jesus' ministry, we may think that we are protecting Protestantism from falling into old "Catholic" habits of elevating her beyond what Scripture declares about her. But there's nothing "Protestant" about neglecting what Scripture does say about her—and about the other women named by the New Testament writers.

Other developments include the founding of the Ecumenical Society of the Blessed Virgin Mary in the United Kingdom in 1967. The ESBVM has brought together Christians from diverse denominations to explore their common interest in the Mother of

Jesus through conferences, books and other publications. Notable anthologies produced by the ESBVM include *Mary's Place in Christian Dialogue*, *Mary and the Churches*, *Mary in Doctrine and Devotion*, *Mary for Everyone*, *Mary for Earth and Heaven* and *Mary for Time and Eternity*.

In parallel with the operation of the ESBVM, the last fifty years saw the publication of three of the most powerful books on Marian doctrine and devotion – all from Protestants. These were Evangelical John de Satge's *Down to Earth: The New Protestant View of the Virgin Mary* (1976), Methodist Neville Ward's *Five for Sorrow, Ten for Joy: A Consideration of the Rosary* (1973) and Anglican John Macquarrie's *Mary for all Christians* (1991).

A few examples of the rediscovery of Marian doctrines by noted Protestant thinkers are cited below.

Robert W. Jenson, Lutheran

> Mary's womb is of course a space. And if she is the Mother of God, if what was in her womb was God the Son, then indeed her womb was the container of the uncontainable; then it is indeed her womb that provides space in our space for the gestating God the Son.
>
> The theological question about Mary's unique place among the holy ones can thus, I suggest, be pointed to a question about God's space in our world. For of no other single person can it be said that he or she contains the uncontainable God.
>
> …
>
> [I]f God is to have to do with his created world and not just coexist with it, and especially if he is also to allow creatures to have to do with him, he needs space in his creation from which to be present to other spaces therein and at which to allow creatures to locate him" … [The Ark of the Covenant, the Temple, the Scrolls of Torah, the Prophets, and the

people themselves are a "space" that God creates to take up residence among us.] It is the space taken up, defined, by the people of Israel, which is, with sheer heaven, God's space in this world. …

It is of course the heart of Christian faith that God's presence in Israel is gathered up and concentrated in Immanuel, God with us, in this one Israelite's presence in Israel: he is in person the Temple's Shekinah, and the Word spoken by all the prophets, and the Torah. And if that is so, then the space delineated by Israel to accommodate the presence of God is finally reduced and expanded to Mary's womb, the container of Immanuel.

We must note the singularity of Mary's dogmatic title: she is not one in a series of God's mothers, she is simply the Mother.

To what did Mary, after all, assent, when she said to Gabriel, "Fiat mihi," "Let it happen to me"? Of course it was her womb that with these words she offered, to be God's space in the world. The whole history of Israel had been God's labor to take Israel as his space in the world. And it indeed was a labor, for Israel by her own account was a resistant people: again and again the Lord's angel announced his advent, begged indeed for space, and again and again Israel's answer was "Let it be, but not yet." Gabriel's mission to Mary was, so to speak, one last try, and this time the response did not temporize. …

As the created space for God, Mary is Israel concentrated. Ancient hymns directly apostrophize her as "the Ark of the Covenant," by an analogy so obvious that it is more than an analogy. When God's creating Word came in its own singular identity into the world, Mary brought him forth as though she were all the prophets put together—indeed, "as though" is not a strong enough way to put it. And if Christianity does not quite reverence the Book as Judaism reverences the Torah-scroll, it is perhaps because its role has been preempted by Mary's act as Torah's embodiment.

When we ask Mary to pray for us, why would we do this specifically in her capacity as Mother of God? …

From the beginning of creation, heaven is God's space in his creation. As the created space for God, there must be a mysterious sense in which Mary is heaven, the container not only of the uncontainable Son, but of all his sisters and brothers, of what Augustine called the *totus Christus*, the whole Christ, Christ with his body. But Mary is a person, not a sheer container. That she contains the whole company of heaven must mean that she personally is their presence. To ask Mary to pray for us is to ask "the whole company of heaven" to pray for us, not this saint or that but all of them together. It is to ask the church triumphant to pray for us.[22]

Beverly Gaventa, Baptist

In Luke's Gospel, at the Annunciation to Mary, Luke also announces what becomes a (perhaps even the) central theme of his two volumes: "Nothing will be impossible with God" (1:37 NRSV). Mary's response signals her consent to the role of the Mother of Jesus. In addition, it identifies another central theme, that of the consent of human beings to God's will. When she consents to God's will, Mary becomes the Mother of Believers…

In the exchange between Gabriel and Mary, we see Mary as the recipient of the gospel's central claim and not only as the first disciple but as the mother of disciples. …

What does it mean to say that Mary is the Mother of Believers, especially in the context of the Lukan story? First, it implies that one of the "things that have been accomplished among us," to go back to Luke's opening lines, is the creation of a new household. Just as Mary understands herself as a slave in God's household, believers become part of that same household. …

The Magnificat takes Mary's "maternal thinking" beyond the life of her own child to encompass the well-being of other children. … She expresses concern for the protection, the well-being, the good will of God's children; in a sense, rhetorically, she takes them for her own.[23]

David S. Yeago, Lutheran

Mary is present within the redemptive relationship of the church and of the believer to Christ by virtue of her presence in the scriptural testimony to Christ. … It is important first to register the fact of her presence as a theologically significant personage. It is here, I believe, that we touch on the root of what I have called the ancient "Marian consciousness" of the church, the awareness of Mary as a singular presence within the mystery of salvation. *The church's awareness of Mary as a presence in the mystery of salvation arises from the church's confession that the real and only savior is the scriptural Christ,* "Jesus Christ as he is attested for us in Holy Scripture." A Christ without Mary, a Christ in whose presence Mary is not also present would be some Christ than the scriptural Christ, the construct of some variety of "*gnosis* falsely called." …

Mary is present to the church and to the believer both as the *prototype* and *model* of the church and the believer, and also as an *active agent* of the formation of the church and the believer. …

Her miraculous pregnancy is embedded in a drama, a narrative in which she is not only object but also subject, playing a part that engages her whole person. She is addressed by the messenger of God, promised that the child to which she shall give birth will be the Son of the Most High. Mary therefore does not figure in the story of salvation only through the bare fact of her pregnancy; her pregnancy is located within a context of covenant and communion, of God's election and promise, and the faith that these evoke. Her role is therefore designed also by the distinctive way in which she *consents* to God's redemptive design, and to her vocation within that design.[24]

John De Satge, Evangelical

I believe that just as we may see in the theological life of the Virgin Mary, as the Scriptures describe her, a model of justification by faith so we may view the beginning and the end of her story which later traditions, held in different ways by Eastern Orthodox and Roman Catholic have added on to the scriptural deposit, not a distortion from it, but as congruent with it and so as legitimate extensions.[25]

Neville Ward, Methodist

It does seem clear that the first-century people who put together the four gospels found that they could not do justice to the mixture of the divine and human in Jesus without saying some very remarkable things about his mother. Their minds were continually drawn to her. Because they felt that to Jesus was given the name that is above every other name, these early Christians sensed an extraordinary mystery about her. They knew as well as we do that the influence of a mother over a child is absolutely incalculable for good or ill. If Jesus was who they thought he was, then who was she?

The earliest Christian communities did not stay long in this realm of question and mystery. Very soon they found themselves surrounding Mary's memory and her presence in the communion of saints with a unique love and thankfulness. Nowadays the birth and infancy narratives, dated in the first century by scholars, are seen as a kind of paean of praise to God and to Mary for Jesus. Since then there has poured through the life of the Christian church an amazing flood of gratitude and love for her whose existence was the slender thread on which, for believers, hangs so much of life's joy and meaning.[26]

The Immaculate Conception

Donald Dawe, Presbyterian

Now predestination always embraces all the necessary graces to accomplish the end of the divine election. In the case of Mary, this implies those graces needed to prepare her for her role as the *Theotokos.* The dogma of the Immaculate Conception is then, according to Nicolas, the explication of what is implied in the election of Mary. Such an analysis holds great promise for fresh interpretations of the Immaculate Conception. [27]

John Macquarrie, Anglican

One could argue that the dogma of the Immaculate Conception is so far from encouraging any Pelagianism that it stands rather as a barrier in the way; for the dogma teaches that the divine grace was present from the very first (prevenient) and that Mary's place is due not to her own merit but to the gracious election and calling that look toward the incarnation of the Son. [28]

The Assumption

Donald Dawe, Presbyterian

The lines of an ecumenical reinterpretation of the dogma of the Assumption of the Blessed Virgin Mary may be traced historically. The basis of ecumenical interpretation is in the unique role of Mary in the history of salvation. She was the one who was graced by the Spirit and able to say 'yes' to the divine Word. So she bore the Saviour and is confessed as Theotokos. But Mary shared in more than the birth of Jesus. Mary is part of the ongoing history of salvation that reaches its fulfillment in the kingdom of God. She is the one who will ultimately be called 'blessed' by 'all generations.' In the life of the people of God, there was a growing awareness of Mary as the one who had already entered fully into the salvation of body and soul for which all long. Mary became a sign of hope to the community of faith. It is the reality of this hope that is celebrated in the Assumption of the blessed Virgin. [29]

John Macquarrie, Anglican

The criticism is sometimes put forward that the dogma of the Assumption is a glorification of Mary, even an apotheosis, which has the result of infringing the place that belongs to Jesus Christ alone. But, rightly understood, it is in no sense independent – as I have said, it is a corollary of Christ's ascension, and if it has been incorporated into the Church's teaching in the course of the development of doctrine, this must be because it has been believed to be an implicate of Christ's ascension. [30]

Charles Dickson, Lutheran

Luther referred to Mary as "God's workshop" and went on to say, "As the Mother of God, she is raised above the whole of humankind" and "has no equal." Contrast this with the modern Protestant attitude that criticizes Marian devotion in the belief that it detracts from the central and unique place Christ occupies in human salvation and you begin to get a picture of the current crisis of division.

What Protestants have had difficulty understanding are the intentions of Catholic teachings about Mary. In the Immaculate Conception and the Assumption teachings it has not been the intention of the Catholic Church to elevate the Blessed Virgin Mary to deity status but rather to show her as the shining model of genuinely Christian hope. It is the hope for all humankind. Such a rereading and enlightened understanding on the part of the Protestant community will help to refocus the attention of the entire Christian world on Mary, not as a point of division, but as the real bridge to unity for us all.[31]

#5 MOTHER OF THE WITNESSES

A Return to Roots

"Is Christ only to be adored? Or is the holy Mother of God rather not to be honoured? This is the woman who crushed the Serpent's head. Hear us. For your Son denies you nothing." Martin Luther, Last Sermon at Wittenberg, January 1546. [1]

Mary – What Christians Today are Called to Do

Action	Bible	Faathers	Councils	Liturgies
Honor	✔	✔	✔	✔
Venerate	✔	✔	✔	✔
Enter into filial relationship	✔	✔	✔	✔
Seek intercession	✔	✔	✔	✔

How is all that we have seen so far relevant to us? If Mary is indeed the All-Holy, Ever-Virgin Mother of God now in Heaven, what difference does this make to a Christian today? The answer was evident to Christians from the beginning. She is our Mother seeking to help us on our journey home to Heaven, interceding for all who ask in our affairs on earth. Here we will drill deeper into this (sometimes controversial) dimension of mediation that is personally relevant to all of us.

As we have reiterated, *Revelation* 12 shows Mary as the mother of all "who obey God's commandments and bear witness to Jesus." (12:17). She is the divinely appointed and scripturally documented mother of all Christians and like any other mother comes to the aid of her children when they are in need – as the faithful have recognized throughout Christian history.

This is why her mediation and intercession have always been understood as maternal.

But this ancient affirmation of Marian mediation has created a yawning chasm between the historic Christian consensus and certain later theories. The Protestant Reformers accepted Mary's divine maternity, personal holiness aond perpetual virginity yet rejected any kind of Marian mediation.

Quite obviously, abuses and excesses in popular Marian devotion need to be corrected. But this wholesale rejection of Mary's continuing role in the history of salvation flies in the face of the Christianity of the Apostles, martyrs, catacombs, Fathers and Councils. Further, many of today's Protestant Fundamentalists seem to reject even the Marian doctrines accepted by the Reformers.

Fortunately, other Protestant Christians – Evangelicals, Methodists, Episcopalians, Lutherans, Presbyterians, Pentecostals, Baptists – are re-discovering the inextricable presence of the Virgin Mother at the heart of salvation history.

We should note, nevertheless, that dissension over Marian mediation takes us to a more fundamental issue. More controversial than the role of Mary in Christian belief is the question of salvation itself. It is no exaggeration to say that wars have been fought over this issue since it was the single most important disagreement that led to the Protestant Reformation and the subsequent division of Christian Europe.

But, in the present day, numerous conferences and ecumenical groups have created a friendlier climate. For instance, there are Anglican-Catholic, Lutheran-Catholic and Evangelical-Catholic dialogues and other such initiatives studying areas of agreement and disagreement. The joint statements from these dialogues have at least created a better understanding of the conflicting positions.

It is commonly agreed by Catholics and Protestants that salvation was given by Jesus Christ and accepted in faith by the believer, that God's grace takes primacy over every human initiative and that we are able to live as the children of God only because of the gift of the Holy Spirit. Disagreement begins over the question of whether or not our freedom plays a role in our salvation.

But this is not a disagreement between Catholics and Orthodox, on the one side, and Protestants on the other. Its roots reach down to two entirely different views of God and humankind and subsequently two different understandings of a wide range of biblical verses. On the one side you have the Calvinists and other determinists and on the other you have Catholics, Orthodox, Protestants from various denominations (like the Methodists) and movements (Pentecostals) and all those who believe in human freedom. Calvinism is not the standard position even among Protestant Evangelicals as illustrated by the anthology of Evangelical scholars titled *The Grace of God, The Will of Man.*

The parting of the ways centers on an issue that is central to this book, namely the question of whether or not we can say "yes" or "no" to God. To the Calvinists "No" was never an option for those whom God has decided to save and when he offers them his grace, his offer is irresistible. The human response is entirely a divinely ordained action and so no merit attaches to it. This means that those whom God has not foreordained for salvation have been foreordained for damnation.

Unlike the Calvinist position, the historic Christian consensus is that God is an infinite Lover who thirsts for every human soul, that he moves Heaven and Earth to make salvation available to his creatures, that he gives every person sufficient grace to say *fiat*, "yes", to him. We can say "yes" to God because of the grace he gives us to say "yes." But we can also say "no" – and this is a free act. The power to say "no" is a negative power we have: one we own. All positive powers are from God. To say "yes" is the greatest, most praiseworthy decision of our lives – one which will bring us endless joy. We look to all those who have said "yes'" as models who motivate us and the greatest of these models is the maiden whose "yes" made her mother of her Savior.

The historic Christian insight into the importance of this "one thing about Mary" is the understanding of biblical teaching that we find professed and proclaimed by the apostolic community and the Church Fathers and Councils.

At this point, we will consider in some detail the questions relating to freedom, salvation, mediation and intercession.

Freedom and Salvation

Predestination to Salvation and Damnation vs. Freedom of the Human Person

The Calvinist, determinist view was well summarized by John Calvin himself in his "Predestination of Some to Salvation and Others to Destruction": "All things being at God's disposal, and the decision of salvation or death belonging to him, he orders all things by his counsel and decree in such a manner, that some men are born devoted from the womb to certain death, that his name may be glorified in their destruction. ... No one can deny that God foreknew the future final fate of man before he created him, and that he did foreknow it because it was appointed by his own decree."[1] "The wicked themselves have been created for this very end – that they may perish."[2]

Martin Luther adopted the Calvinist view although he was clearly troubled by it: "Doubtless it gives the greatest possible offence to common sense or natural reason, that God, Who is proclaimed as being full of mercy and goodness, and so on, should of His own mere will abandon, harden, and damn men, as though He delighted in the sins and great eternal torments of such wretches. ... I have stumbled at it myself more than once, down to the deepest pit of despair."[3]

The historic Christian response to this line of thought was well summed up by John Wesley in his "Predestination Calmly Considered," the most extraordinary extant refutation of Calvinism, "Now if man be capable of choosing good or evil, then is he a proper object of the justice of God, acquitting or condemning, rewarding or punishing. But otherwise he is not. A mere machine is not capable of being either acquitted or condemned. Justice cannot punish a stone for falling to the ground. ... And shall this man, for not doing what he never could do, and for doing what he never could avoid, be sentenced to depart into everlasting fire, prepared for the devil and his angels (cf. Mt. 25:41)? 'Yes, because it is the sovereign will of God.' Then you either found a new God, or made one! This is not the God of the Christians. Our God is just in all his ways. … He requireth only according to what he hath given; and where he hath given little, little is required. The glory of his justice is this, to 'reward every man according to his works.' (cf. Tm 4:14)."[4]

The Council of Orange had declared in 529 "We not only do not believe that any are foreordained to evil by the power of God, but even state with utter abhorrence that if there are those who want to believe so evil a thing, they are anathema."

As long as you take the Calvinist view of the matter, which Luther did, there can be no further progression on mediation. But, as John Macquarrie points out, this view is at odds of both human experience and Christian doctrine and experience because it treats "human beings like sheep or cattle or even marionettes, not as the unique beings that they are, spiritual beings made in the image of God and entrusted with a measure of freedom and responsibility."[5]

The main foundation for the doctrine that our free decisions determine our eternal destiny is the teaching of Jesus:
> "And there was a man who came to him and asked, 'Master, what good deed must I do to possess eternal life?' Jesus said to him, '… If you wish to enter into life, keep the commandments. … If you wish to be perfect, go and sell what you own and give the money to the poor, and you will have treasure in heaven; then come, follow me.'" (*Matthew* 19:16-22).
>
> "For every unfounded word men utter they will answer on Judgment day, since it is by your words you will be acquitted, and by your words condemned." (*Matthew* 12:37)
>
> "In his anger the master handed him over to the torturers till he should pay all his debt. And that is how my heavenly Father will deal with you unless you each forgive your

brother from your heart." (*Matthew* 18:34-5).

"You will be hated by all men on account of my name; but the man who stands firm to the end will be saved." (*Matthew* 10:22).

"For the Son of Man is going to come in the glory of his Father with his angels, and, when he does, he will reward each one according to his behavior." (*Matthew* 16:27)

"I tell you solemnly, in so far as you neglected to do this to one of the least of these, you neglected to do it to me.' And they will go away to eternal punishment, and the virtuous to eternal life." (*Matthew* 25:45-6).

"The hour is coming when the dead will leave their graves at the sound of his voice; those who did good will rise again for life; and those who did evil, to condemnation." (*John* 5:28-8).

In the book of *Revelation*, Jesus says, "Very soon now, I shall be with you again, bringing the reward to be given to every man according to what he deserves." (*Revelation* 22:12).

Some have said that any attempt to focus on being good and holy is a deception of the Devil who tries to make us rely on our own good works for our salvation instead of focusing only on the all-sufficient atonement of Jesus.

While affirming that salvation is possible only because of the redemptive death of Jesus and that we cannot be saved unless he draws us to him and gives us the grace to accept him, we could just as plausibly say that any attempt to downplay the need for holiness and for turning away from sin is a deception of the Devil who wants to lead us from trivial sins to the terrible fate of which we are warned in *Hebrews*: "If, after we have been given knowledge of the truth, we should deliberately commit any sins, then there is no longer any sacrifice for them. There will be left only the dread prospect of judgment and of the raging fire that is to burn rebels. Anyone who disregards the Law of Moses is ruthlessly put to death on the word of two witnesses or three; and you may be sure that anyone who tramples on the Son of God and treats the blood of the covenant which sanctified him as if it were not holy, and who insults the Spirit of grace, will be condemned to a far severer punishment." (*Hebrews* 10:26-30).

The Apostle Paul has a similar warning: "Your stubborn refusal to repent is only adding to the anger God will have toward you on that day of anger when his just judgments will be made known. He will repay each one as his works deserve. For those who sought renown and honor and immortality by always doing good there will be eternal life; for the unsubmissive who refused to take truth for their guide and tookd depravity instead, there will be anger and fury." (*Romans* 2:5-8).

Moreover, the followers of Jesus participate in His work of salvation. As Paul said, through his bodily suffering, he does what he can "to make up all that has still to be undergone by Christ for the sake of his body, the Church." (*Colossians* 1:24). The Apostle James even says that "Anyone who can bring back a sinner from the wrong way that he has taken will be saving a soul from death and covering up a great number of sins." (*James* 5:20).

To recap what was said earlier, Mary is a key participant in God's plan of salvation in human history. She was called to be the Mother of the Savior and to share in His salvific suffering; it was her *fiat* ("Let it be done") to the messenger from God that made the Incarnation possible; she played a key role in the miracle that began His ministry in the world; she was there with Him at the end of His life; and she was called to be the Mother of all those who witness to Jesus. As the Witness who is the Mother of all witnesses, she is a human expression of the infinite love of God that seeks the salvation of every soul. When she tells us about coming to her Son and about her maternal protection she is speaking to us a mother seeking the well-being of her children.

Mediation

Mediators in the Old and New Testaments

Both Old and New Testaments not only show the significance of our free acts but the very real role of mediators in God's scheme of salvation. Adam, Noah, Abraham and Moses, the Prophets, Judges and Kings of the Old Testaments, were all mediators between God and humanity. Their free actions could bring divine blessings on their people. They could cause or avert God's wrath. Things are no different in the New Testament. The Apostles and disciples are chosen and commissioned to spread the Good News, to bring people to salvation, to celebrate the sacred mysteries that "transmit" the grace of God. And we have already mentioned *Colossians* 1:24.

The One Mediator

1 *Timothy* 2:5 says, "There is only one mediator between God and mankind, himself a man, Christ Jesus, who sacrificed himself as a ransom for them all." Does "one" here mean "exclusively one" or does it mean "the same" and by extension "primary"? Interestingly, the Greek word used for "exclusively one", *monos*, is used in every other instance of "one" in the epistle except in this verse. The word used here is *"heis"* where it means "sameness" of function. In his study of *Timothy* 2:5, "For there is one God, and one mediator between God and men, the man Christ Jesus; Who gave himself a ransom for all," Manuel Miguens points out that an accurate translation of this passage is "There is one and the same God [for all], there is also one and the same mediator [for all]." The author is not trying to show that there is one and not a multiplicity of gods or that there is one and not many mediators. His point, rather, is that God's love and providence applies to all not just to a few (the Jews, for instance) just as the redemptive mediation of Jesus is for all. In his epistles, St. Paul, of course, talks of himself as a mediator and even talks of three kinds of mediators: priestly (Aaron, Christ),

covenantal (Moses, Jesus) and de facto mediators (Abraham and Paul). The last category comprises those chosen to be vehicles of divine grace. The mediation of all Christians (as described in *Colossians* 1:24 and elsewhere) is a participation in the unique and primary mediation of Christ. He alone is the unique Son of God – but all Christians can and must participate in this Sonship as they can and must participate in His unique Priesthood. So also, all are called to participate in the unique mediation of the Primary Mediator. All followers of Jesus participate in his work of salvation. "We are co-workers with God," said Paul.

Maternal Mediation

Given that Christians are co-workers with Christ and hence mediators of salvation and God's grace, how are we to understand the role of the Mother of the Lord?

We have seen that the Blessed Virgin was always seen as the New Eve.

Macquarrie notes that, "In the glimpses of Mary that we have in the gospels, her standing at the cross beside her Son, and her prayers and intercessions with the apostles, are particularly striking ways in which Mary shared and supported the work of Christ …. But it is Mary who has come to symbolize that perfect harmony between the divine will and the human response … Her contribution was unique and by its very nature could not be literally shared with anyone else. We are thinking of her now not just as representative or pre-eminent member of the Church, but as Theotokos or Mother of God. Mary's willing acceptance of her indispensable role in that chain of events which constituted the incarnation and the redemption which it brought about, was necessary for the nurture of the Lord and for the creation of the Church itself."[6]

And just as her participation in the work of the One Redeemer is qualitatively different from the participation of other participants in the work entrusted by Christ, her maternal mediation is qualitatively different from the way in which other mediators participate in her Son's mediation. Jesus is the unique and unrepeatable Redeemer and Mediator. He is God and man. But all Christians are called to participate in his redemptive activity and his mediation – and the first to do so was the New Eve who was uniquely also *Theotokos* (Mother of God). Her mediation also arises from the biblically recorded uniqueness of her union with the Holy Spirit (*Panagia*) which was acknowledged and celebrated by the Christian community from the beginning.

The mediation of Mary, to repeat, is intrinsically maternal in nature: she is the most perfect created image of the Father because only the Father and Mary have generated the Son and by her cooperation in the Incarnation she "mediates" the Redeemer of fallen humanity; she is also mother of all those who witness to Christ (*Revelation* 12:17) for those who participate in the sonship of Christ (*Galatians* 4:4) are adopted sons and daughters of his eternal Father and his human Mother. Even when she is a mediator of her Son's power at Cana, this mediation is maternal in nature and it is a mediation that inspires faith in the Apostles.

The Presbyterian scholar Ross Mackenzie writes, "To bid Mary stand beside us is to remember that we are already with her in the new creation. She is linked with us, and ministers to us still in the new creation as the Mother of mercy. To invoke her in public and private prayer is to recall that, while the first creation came about by the will of God alone, the new creation involved this woman's will also. She is a minister of God, *synergos theou*, to use one of Paul's daring phrases. Even the least of the apostles considered himself linked with Christ in a glorious cause: 'We entreat you on behalf of Christ,' he says to the Corinthians, 'to be reconciled to God,' 2 Cor 5:20. To speak on behalf of Christ, is therefore to be a mediator of God's saving work in the world."[7]

Intercession

Does Mary continue to intercede for us in Heaven? The larger question here concerns whether or not a person in Heaven can affect events on earth. We can address these issues by consideration of five different issues.

1. *Perseverance in prayer is commended in Scripture with the promise that this will achieve results.*
"He said, 'There was a judge in a certain town who neither feared God nor respected any human being. And a widow in that town used to come to him and say, 'Render a just decision for me against my adversary.' For a long time the judge was unwilling, but eventually he thought, 'While it is true that I neither fear God nor respect any human being, because this widow keeps bothering me I shall deliver a just decision for her lest she finally come and strike me.' The Lord said, 'Pay attention to what the dishonest judge says. Will not God the secure the rights of his chosen ones who call out to him day and night? Will he be slow to answer them? I tell you, he will see to it that justice is done for them speedily.'" (*Luke* 18:2-8).

2. *Intercessory prayer from multiple persons will achieve results.*
"Peter thus was being kept in prison, but prayer by the church was fervently being made to God on his behalf." (*Acts* 12:5).

"First of all, then, I ask that supplications, prayers, petitions, and thanksgivings be offered for everyone, for kings and for all in authority, that we may lead a quiet and tranquil life in all devotion and dignity. This is good and pleasing to God our savior, who wills everyone to be saved and to come to knowledge of the truth." (1 *Timothy* 2:1-5).

"As you help us with prayer, so that thanks may be given by many on our behalf for the gift granted us through the prayers of many."

(*2 Corinthians* 1:11).

3. The prayer of a holy person is especially effective

"The fervent prayer of a righteous person is very powerful." (*James* 5:16)

4. The prayer of the Holy Ones in Heaven has an effect on earthly events.

"When he took it, the four living creatures and the twenty-four elders fell down before the Lamb. Each of the elders held a harp and gold bowls filled with incense, which are the prayers of the holy ones." (*Revelation* 5:8). The elders in this instance are Christians in Heaven. "The smoke of the incense along with the prayers of the holy ones went up before God from the hand of the angel." (*Revelation* 8:4). "I saw underneath the altar the souls of those who had been slaughtered because of the witness they bore to the word of God. They cried out in a loud voice, 'How long will it be, holy and true master, before you sit in judgment and avenge our blood on the inhabitants of the earth?' Each of them was given a white robe, and they were told to be patient a little while longer until the number was filled of their fellow servants and brothers who were going to be killed as they had been." (*Revelation* 6:9-11).

The Anglican theologian Edward Symonds observes that "There are other considerations however in favour of the view that the saints hear us. There is actual evidence for this belief in the New Testament. Heb 12:1 says: 'Therefore let us also being compassed about with so great a cloud of witnesses ("martyrs", alluding to the heroes of faith in the preceding chapter) run with patience ("endurance") the race which is set before us', where the witnesses, though primarily witnesses to their faith suggest at least, as Westcott points out, 'spectators' looking on at our earthly struggle in running the race appointed for us Christians. This is confirmed by the picture of the heavenly Jerusalem in the same chapter to which Christians on earth are now come, with the solemn assembly of the firstborn and the spirits of just men made perfect. (Verse 23)."[8]

Noted Lutheran theologian **Robert W. Jenson** explains why

invoking the saints is possible and desirable:

> It has long seemed plain to this Protestant that the invocation of saints' prayers must be possible and if possible surely desirable. I certainly can ask a living fellow believer to pray for me. If death severed the fellowship of believers, I could not of course ask a departed fellow believer to pray for me. But the New Testament hardly permits us to think that death can sever the fellowship of believers — and the eucharistic prayers also of Protestant bodies explicitly deny that it does. Thus there seems to be no reason why I cannot ask also a departed believer to pray for me. And if I can do it, there will certainly be contexts where I should do it. Thus there should be no problem about asking Mary in her capacity as sancta, Saint Mary, to pray for us.

Those of the Reformers who thought otherwise needed to produce more stringent arguments than any I am aware of their adducing. Simply saying with Melanchthon that there is no scriptural mandate to address individual saints, will not do. Magisterial Protestant churches live by all kinds of practices, perhaps most notably infant baptism and the authority of the New Testament canon, for which no scriptural mandate exists, and which can be justified only by chains of argument far longer than the one just developed for invoking saints. On infant baptism Luther's final word was simply that this had long been the practice of the church, and that he saw no decisive argument against it. One must wonder why the same cannot be said about invocation of the saints.[9]

The Intercession of the Mother of God

Of all the saints in Heaven, it is the mediation of the Mother of all saints that is the most powerful. She is the daughter who "found favor" with the Father, the New Eve who intercedes with the New Adam whose "hour" has now come, the Spouse of the Spirit of God who said of her "blessed are you who believed." She is the Queen-Mother "clothed with the sun" who intercedes on behalf of "her offspring, those who keep God's commandments and bear witness to Jesus." (*Revelation* 12).

It was Mary's compassionate request that led to her Son's first miracle at the beginning of his Ministry - and so Mary's intercession especially as it relates to miracles was widely accepted.

Symonds points out that, "Mary is recognized as the mother of all Christian people from at least the time of Origen, who says, 'No one will be able to understand the meaning of St John's Gospel if he has not leaned on the breast of Jesus and received from Jesus the one who has become his mother also. Because Christ lives in him, the words are said to Mary of him, 'Behold thy Son the Christ.' This motherhood is perpetual, for the Incarnation is a permanent reality not a merely past event. Our Lord retains his human Nature in Heaven. Therefore Mary is still his Mother, but also the Mother of the Church which is his Body, the living organism of Christ's glorified human Nature and of each of its members, who are made her adopted, not her natural children, by their baptismal incorporation into the human Nature of her Son. But a further question is, how does our Lady exercise this motherhood? The answer is by love, and by intercession. There can be no doubt that the saints exercise charity, the crown of Christian virtues, in Heaven. And that charity which is primarily directed towards God is, as the New Testament teaches, empty and worthless if it does not include the love of man, specially of our fellow-members in the Body of Christ. And this love finds its chief (though not its only) expression, in the case of the saints in Heaven, in intercession."[10]

This is the historic Christian consensus about Marian mediation that echoes through ancient prayers and liturgies, councils and creeds, doctrines and devotions. To the question of why we cannot pray directly to God, the reply is that we can and do – but also that prayers to the saints ultimately results in prayers that go directly to God from them. If we can legitimately ask our friends to pray for us why can we not ask the Holy Ones in Heaven to pray for us? We remember that "The fervent prayer of a righteous person is very powerful," that the "the spirits of righteous men made perfect" are in Heaven (*Hebrews* 12:23), and these spirits are very much alive since our God is "not the God of the dead but of the living." (*Matthew* 22:32).

Admittedly these approaches to mediation and intercession are incompatible with a strict reading of the Reformation writings. Nevertheless, much progress has been made on justification, the major theological issue of the Reformation. In their landmark 1999 Joint Declaration on the Doctrine of Justification, the Lutheran World Federation and the Catholic Church concluded, "The understanding of the doctrine of justification set forth in this Declaration shows that a consensus in basic truths of the doctrine of justification exists between Lutherans and Catholics." Professor Tadeusz Zielinksy of the Baptist World Alliance noted on December 5, 2003, that the doctrine of justification in the Joint Declaration (nn.14-18) "can be … endorsed by all Baptists without hesitation. Those paragraphs [nn.19,22,31,34,37] showing the Lutheran-Catholic consensus [deserve] full Baptist support."

Ongoing dialogues between Catholics and Lutherans, Methodists, Anglicans and other denominations on the subject of mediation, and in particular Marian mediation, have helped eliminate some misconceptions. The 2005 declaration from the Anglican-Catholic dialogue (ARCIC) titled *Mary: Grace and Hope in Christ* is of particular importance: "Affirming together unambiguously Christ's unique mediation, which bears fruit in the life of the Church, we do not consider the practice of asking Mary and the saints to pray for us as communion-dividing. Since obstacles of the past have been removed by clarification of doctrine, by liturgical reform and practical norms in keeping with it, we believe that there is no continuing theological reason for ecclesial division on these matters."

On the way forward, Methodist David Butler's recommendations seem to be specially relevant: "Protestants need to receive what they already have espoused theologically, in terms of Mary as a type of the true believer, one who offered her 'let it be' to God in faith and thereby becomes an example of how we must act. They need to unpack for themselves the implications of the title offered at Ephesus 431 of *Theotokos*, or Mother of God, for Marian devotion. After all, Protestants acknowledge the fundamental principles of the historic creeds, and the Council of Ephesus 431 safeguards the humanity of Christ. Perhaps this preliminary work, which is devotional as much as it is doctrinal, will enable them to see the value of the definitions of 1854 and 1950."[11]

The significance of Mary is above all as a link to her Son. The fundamental driving force of all Marian doctrine and devotion is the perception that it is only through her we can fully accept and appreciate both his divinity and his humanity. Her divine maternity – human mother of God the Son – is the most telling testimony to his true humanity. Her special status – immaculately conceived, perpetually virgin, assumed into Heaven, New Eve – presupposes and confirms his divinity.

We know too that in the entire Bible, only two human persons beheld God in his Supernatural Splendor: Moses on Mount Sinai and Mary who was "overshadowed" by the Holy Spirit. Both said "Yes" to God with respect to their specific missions. But whereas Moses, like Abraham, was tasked with "forming" the People of God, Mary was called to become the Mother of God and Mother of the People of God.

Postscript

Our inquiry reveals that the story of Mary, the Mother of Jesus, in its entirety is organically inextricable from the Christian message. The apostolic community affirmed it, the Fathers taught it, the Councils proclaimed it, the first liturgies testified to it and the faithful lived it. A Christianity without the ever-Virgin, All-Holy, Mother of God interceding for us from Heaven is not the Christianity of the first-century and first-millennium Christians. Without her consent to God – the one thing above all for which we honor and emulate her – there would have been no Incarnation and no salvation. And it is God who gifted her to us as our Mother. It is now we who have to give our "Yes" to the gift. We can avail ourselves of this gift from the Giver of all "perfect gifts" or simply return it unopened to its Sender. But remember this: if we are to become children of the Father, we must become brothers and sisters of the Son. And if we are to become a brother or sister of Jesus, we must consent to becoming a child of his Mother.

NOTES

INTRODUCTION

[1]Willie Jennings in Jason Byassee, "Protestants and Marian Devotion—What about Mary?" https://www.religion-online.org/article/protestants-and-marian-devotion-what-about-mary/.

[2] David S. Yeago, "The Presence of Mary in the Mystery of the Church," in *Mary, Mother of God*, Carl E. Bratten and Robert W. Jenson, eds. (Grand Rapids, Michigan: Wm. B. Eerdmans, 2004), 72.

[3]Friedrich Heiler, "Die Gottesmutter im Glauben und Beten der Jahrhunderte," Hochkirche 13 (1931), 200.

[4]Basilea Schlink, *Mary, the Mother of Jesus* (London: Marshall Pickering, 1986), 114-115.

[5]Allan Lancashire, *Born of the Virgin Mary* (London: The Faith Press, 1962), 142-3.

[6]Robert W. Jenson, "A Space for God," in *Mary, Mother of God*, Carl E. Bratten and Robert W. Jenson, eds. (Grand Rapids, Michigan: Wm. B. Eerdmans, 2004), 56.

#1 WHAT THE BIBLE SAYS

How

#1 No Authoritative Interpretation

[1]Michael Cahill, "An Uncertain Jesus: Theological and Scholarly Ambiguities", *Irish Theological Quarterly*, Volume 1, 1998, 28.

[2]Charlotte Allen, *The Human Christ: The Search for the Historical Jesus* (New York: The Free Press, 1998), 6.

#2 One Authoritative Interpretation

[3]https://www.thegospelcoalition.org/themelios/article/history-theology-and-the-biblical-canon-an-introduction-to-basic-issues/

[4]Timothy George, "The Blessed Virgin Mary in Evangelical Perspective," in *Mary, Mother of God*, Carl E. Bratten and Robert W. Jenson, eds. (Grand Rapids, Michigan: Wm. B. Eerdmans, 2004), 117-8.

What
Her Words

⁵Ralph Russell, "The Blessed Virgin Mary in the Bible," in *Mary's Place in Christian Dialogue*, Alberic Stacpoole, ed. (Slough, England: St. Paul Publications, 1983), 48.

Words About Her
"Kecharitomene" – "Our tainted nature's solitary boast"

⁶Blass and DeBrunner, *Greek Grammar of the New Testament*, Chicago: University of Chicago Press, 1961), 175.

⁷A. T. Robertson, *Word Pictures in the New Testament* (Nashville: Broadman Press, 1930), vol. 2, 13.

⁸Herbert Weir Smyth, *Greek Grammar* (Harvard University Press, 1968), 108–109.

⁹Ignace de la Potterie, *Mary in the Mystery of the Covenant* (New York: Alba House, 1992), 17-20.

¹⁰http://philomenarocks.blogspot.com/2013/04/hwp-hail-kecharitomene.html

¹¹Origen, PG 13, 1815-1816.

The Mother of My Lord"

¹²Brant Pitre, *Jesus and the Jewish Roots of Mary* (New York: Image, 2018), 92-3.

"A Woman Clothed with the Sun"

¹³https://www.catholicworldreport.com/2020/09/07/what-does-the-bible-really-say-about-mary-the-mother-of-the-messiah/

¹⁴https://catholicproductions.com/blogs/blog/revelation-12-and-mary-queen-of-heaven

¹⁵Cited in Brant Pitre, *Jesus and the Jewish Roots of Mary* (New York: Image, 2018), 33.

¹⁶Ibid., 23.

#2 WHAT THE NEW TESTAMENT APOSTOLIC COMMUNITY PROCLAIMED

New Eve, Queen-Mother, Mother of Emmanuel, All-Holy Ark of the Covenant, Intercessory Mother of the Faithful, Virgin Mary

[1] http://www.rapturenotes.com/mary.html

[2] John F. Murphy in *Mariology*, Volume 3, Juniper P. Carol ed. (Milwaukee, Wisconsin: The Bruce Publishing Company), 3.

[3] Jaroslav Pelikan, *Mary Through the Centuries: Her Place in the History of Culture* (New Haven and London: Yale University Press, 1996), p. 43.

[4] Citations from Bertrand Buby, *The Marian Heritage of the Early Church* (New York: Alba House, 1996), Peter Brookby ed. *Virgin Wholly Marvellous* (Cambridge: The Ravengate Press, 1981) and other sources.

[5] *Early Christian Doctrines* (San Francisco: HarperCollins, 1978), 493-494.

[6] *History of the Christian Church*, Vol. III: Nicene and Post-Nicene Christianity: A.D. 311-600, (Grand Rapids, Michigan: Eerdmans, 1974). 414-415.

[7] https://www.catholicworldreport.com/2020/09/07/what-does-the-bible-really-say-about-mary-the-mother-of-the-messiah/

[8] https://aleteia.org/2018/11/01/a-jewish-perspective-on-the-queen-of-all-these-saints-were-celebrating/

The queenship of Mary prefigured in Isaiah 7 and shown in Matthew 1 and Revelation 12 is different in kind from pagan ideas of goddesses and queens of heaven. As Pitre writes, "The New Testament does depict Mary as a queen – but not the pagan 'Queen of Heaven.' Instead it depicts as the queen mother of the Messiah's kingdom. In ancient Israel, it was not the king's wife who was queen but his mother … [In ancient times] a crown was the symbol of royal identity and authority. In the case of Revelation 12, this is indisputable, since the crown consists of "twelve stars" – which clearly symbolize the twelve tribes of Israel (cf. Genesis 37:9-10). Seen in this light, the woman clothed with the sun is nothing less than the queen of the people of God with her crown representing 'a share in Christ's kingship.' … The woman clothed with the sun is standing above the moon and the stars 'in heaven' (Revelation 12:1). Her location matters because it presents a strong parallel with Jesus' being 'caught up' to 'the throne' of God in heaven (Revelation 12:5; cf. 4:2). Just as Jesus is a heavenly king who reigns over a *heavenly* kingdom, so, Mary, Jesus' mother is a *heavenly* queen. According to the portrait of Jesus' mother in the book of Revelation, she can rightly be described as *the queen of the kingdom of heaven. … In sum, when we look at the New Testament in the light of ancient Jewish beliefs about the kings and queens of Israel, we can see very clearly that the mother of Jesus is repeatedly depicted as the queen mother of the kingdom of God.*" Brant Pitre, *Jesus and the Jewish Roots of Mary* (New York: Image, 2018), 10, 87-9.

[9]https://pintpipeandcross.wordpress.com/
the-early-church-fathers-on-mary-the-mother-of-god/

[10]Kallistos of Diokleia, "Sanctity and Glory of the Mother of God – Orthodox Approaches"
https://www.theway.org.uk/back/s051Ware.pdf

[11]http://www.patheos.com/blogs/davearmstrong/2016/05/church-fathers-mary-is-sinless.html)

Gambero, Luigi, *Mary and the Fathers of the Church: The Blessed Virgin Mary in Patristic Thought*, Thomas Buffer, translator, San Francisco: Ignatius Press, revised edition of 1999.

Graef, Hilda, *Mary: A History of Doctrine and Devotion*, vol. 1 [to the Reformation], New York: Sheed and Ward, 1963.

Jurgens, William A., editor and translator, *The Faith of the Early Fathers*, three volumes, Collegeville, Minnesota: Liturgical Press, 1970 and 1979 (2nd and 3rd volumes).

Kelly, J.N.D., *Early Christian Doctrines*, San Francisco: Harper & Row, fifth revised edition, 1978.

O'Carroll, Michael, *Theotokos: A Theological Encyclopedia of the Blessed Virgin Mary*, Wilmington, Delaware: M. Glazier, 1982.

Schaff, Philip & Henry Wace, editors, *Early Church Fathers: Nicene & Post-Nicene Fathers Series 2* ("NPNF 2"), 14 volumes, originally published in Edinburgh, 1900.

[12]http://www.copticchurch.net/topics/liturgy/liturgy_of_st_basil.pdf

[13]https://www.goarch.org/-/the-divine-liturgy-of-saint-john-chrysostom

[14]https://staycatholic.com/ecf-on-mary-mother-of-the-church/

[15]*A Marian Prayer Book: A Treasury of Prayers, Hymns, and Meditations,* edited by Pamela Moran, Ann Arbor, MI: Servant Publications, 1991), 226.

[16]*The Greatest Marian Prayers: Their History, Meaning, and Usage,* Anthony M. Buono, New York: Alba House, 1999), 111.

[17]*A Marian Prayer Book: A Treasury of Prayers, Hymns, and Meditations,* **op cit.,** 76-77.

[18]*The Greatest Marian Prayers: Their History, Meaning, and Usage,* **op cit.,** 112.

[19]https://www.beholdthetruth.com/key-early-historical-writings-on-mary

#3 WHAT ALL FIRST MILLENNIUM CHRISTIANS AFFIRMED
Theotokos (Mother of God), Panagia (All-Holy), Heavenly Intercessor, Aeiparthenos (Ever-Virgin)

[1]https://www.historyofinformation.com/detail.php?id=2662

[2]John F. Murphy, **op cit.**, 4-5.

[3]William Cole. "Was Luther a Devotee of Mary?" (Marian Studies Volume XXI, 1970, p.131).

Appendices

Mother of God?

[4]Eric Mascall, "The Mother of God," in *Mary's Place in Christian Dialogue*, Albert Stacpoole, ed. (Middlegreen, Slough: St. Paul Publications, 1982), 93-5.

[5]Eric L. Mascall, "Theotokos: The Place of Mary in the Work of Salvation," in *The Blessed Virgin Mary: Essays by Anglican Writers*, E.L. Mascall and H.S. Box, eds. (London: Darton, Longman & Todd Ltd, 1963), 14.

[6]Gerald Van Ackeren, "Mary's Divine Motherhood" in *Mariology*, Volume 2, Juniper B. Carol ed. (Milwaukee: The Bruce Publishing Company, 1957), 214.

All-Holy?

[7]Charles Augustus Briggs, *The Incarnation of the Lord* (Charles Scribner's sons, New York, 1902), 215-35.

Assumed into Heaven?

[8]Francis Davis, "Our Lady's Assumption" in *Mother of the Redeemer*, Kevin McNamara, ed. (New York: Sheed and Ward, 1960), 193,195.

[9]Stephen J. Shoemaker, *Ancient Traditions of the Virgin's Mary Dormition and Assumption* (Oxford University Press, 2002), 67–69.

[10]Bernard Lonergan, "The Assumption and Theology," *Collection: Papers by Bernard Lonergan, S.J.,* ed. F. E. Crowe, (New York: Herder and Herder, 1967), 75.

Perpetual Virginity?

[11]Brant Pitre, *Jesus and the Jewish Roots of Mary* (New York: Image, 2018), 116-7.

[12]"The Brothers of Jesus and His Mother's Virginity," *The Thomist* 63, 1999.

[13]David F. Wright, ed., *Chosen by God: Mary in Evangelical Perspective* (London: Marshall Pickering, 1989), 170-1.

[14]Harold Riley, "The Brothers of the Lord," *Downside Review*, January 1998.

[15]H.E. iii:32. Cited in Riley, ibid.

[16]H.E. iii:20.

[17]http://campus.udayton.edu/mary/Rossier.html

[18]Brant Pitre, **op cit**., 105-6.

[19]Gordon Wakefield, "The Methodist Point of View," in *Mother of Jesus* (London: Ecumenical Society for the Blessed Virgin Mary, 1968), 8.

#4 WHAT THE PROTESTANT REFORMERS AND MODERN PROTESTANT THINKERS PROFESSED
All-Holy Virgin Mary, Mother of God, Mother of Believers

[1]Martin Luther, Weimar edition of *Martin Luther's Works*, English translation edited by J. Pelikan (Concordia: St. Louis), volume 24, 107.

[2]Martin Luther, op. cit., Volume 11, 319-320.

[3]Martin Luther, Weimar edition of *Martin Luther's Works*, English translation edited by J. Pelikan (Concordia: St. Louis), Volume 4, 694.

[4]Personal "Little" Prayer Book, 1522.

[5]Martin Luther, Weimar edition of *Martin Luther's Works* (Translation by William J. Cole) 10, 268.

[6]Martin Luther, Weimar edition of *Martin Luther's Works* (Translation by William J. Cole) 10, III, p.313.

[7]Martin Luther, Weimar edition of *Martin Luther's Works*, English translation edited by J. Pelikan [Concordia: St. Louis], Volume 51, 128-129.

[8]John Calvin, *Calvini Opera* [Braunshweig-Berlin, 1863-1900], Volume 45, 35.)

[9]Bernard Leeming, "Protestants and Our Lady", *Marian Library Studies*, January 1967, 9.

[10]George H. Tavard, *The Thousand Faces of Mary* (Michael Glazier), 1996.

[11]Ibid.

[12]John Calvin, *Calvini Opera* [Braunshweig-Berlin, 1863-1900], Volume 45, 348.

[13]John Calvin, *A Harmony of Matthew, Mark and Luke* (St. Andrew's Press, Edinburgh, 1972), 32.

[14]Ulrich Zwingli, *In Evang. Luc., Opera Completa* [Zurich, 1828-42], Volume 6, I, 639.

[15]Ulrich Zwingli, *Zwingli Opera, Corpus Reformatorum*, Volume 1, 424.

[16]E. Stakemeier, *De Mariologia et Oecumenismo*, K. Balic, ed., (Rome, 1962), 456.

[17]Ibid.

[18]Ibid.

[19]Ulrich Zwingli, *Zwingli Opera, Corpus Reformatorum*, Volume 1, 427-428.

[20]David F. Wright, *Chosen by God* (London: Marshall Pickering, 1989), 180.

[21]*Mary for Everyone* edited by William McLoughlin and Jill Pinnock (Herefordshire: Gracewing, 1997, 57.

[22]Robert W. Jenson, "A Space for God," in *Mary, Mother of God*, Carl E.

Bratten and Robert W. Jenson, eds. (Grand Rapids, Michigan: Wm. B. Eerdmans, 2004), 51, 53, 55-6, 57.

[23]Beverly Gaventa, "Nothing will be impossible for God: Mary as the Mother of Believers," in *Mary, Mother of God*, Carl E. Bratten and Robert W. Jenson, eds. (Grand Rapids, Michigan: Wm. B. Eerdmans, 2004), 19, 22-4.

[24]David S. Yeago, "The Presence of Mary in the Mystery of the Church," in *Mary, Mother of God*, Carl E. Bratten and Robert W. Jenson, eds. (Grand Rapids, Michigan: Wm. B. Eerdmans, 2004), 62-3, 65-7.

[25]John de Satge, *Down to Earth: The New Protestant Vision of the Virgin Mary* (Consortium Books, 1976), 112-3.

[26]J. Neville Ward, *Five for Sorrow, Ten for Joy* (Cambridge, MA: Cowley Press, 1985), ix, x.

[27]Donald Dawe, "The Immaculate Conception in Ecumenical Perspective," *The Way*, Number 51, Autumn 1984, 36.

[28]John MacQuarrie, *Mary for all Christians* (London: Collins, 1990), 112.

[29]"The Assumption of the Blessed Virgin in Ecumenical Perspective," *The Way*, Number 45, June 1982, 45.

[30]John MacQuarrie, *Mary for all Christians*, **op cit.**, 82.

[31]Charles Dickson, *A Protestant Pastor Looks at Mary* (Huntington, Indiana: Our Sunday Visitor, 1996), 109-110.

#5 MOTHER OF THE WITNESSES
A Return to Roots

[1]Martin Luther, Weimar edition of *Martin Luther's Works*, English
translation edited by J. Pelikan [Concordia: St. Louis], Volume 51, 128-129.

Freedom and Salvation

[1]John Calvin, *Institutes of the Christian Religion*, Volume II, Philadelphia:
Presbyterian Board of Christian Education.

[2]Citation in John Murray, *Calvin on Scripture and Divine Sovereignty*
(Michigan: Baker Book House, 1960, 61

[3]Martin Luther, *Bondage of the Will*, translated J.I. Packer and O.R. Johnston
(Revell: 1957), 217.

[4]John Wesley, "Predestination Calmly Considered," in Albert C. Outler, ed.
John Wesley (New York: Oxford University Press, 1964), 451.

[5]John MacQuarrie, *Mary for all Christians*, **op. cit.**,104.

[6]Ibid., 113-4.

Mediation

[7]Ross Mackenzie, "Mary: Intercessor on Our Behalf, One with Us in the
Communion of Saints, and Witness to What We May Become in Christ,"
https://ecommons.udayton.edu/marian_studies/vol48/iss1/8/

Intercession

[8]H. Edward Symonds, "The Blessed Virgin Mary," in *The Blessed Virgin
Mary: Essays by Anglican Writers*, E.L. Mascall and H.S. Box, eds. (London:
Darton, Longman & Todd Ltd, 1963), 6-7.

[9]Robert W. Jenson, "A Space for God," in *Mary, Mother of God*, **op cit.**,
49-50.

[10]H. Edward Symonds, **op cit.**, 6.

[11]David Butler in Mary for Everyone edited by William McLoughlin and Jill
Pinnock(Herefordshire: Gracewing, 1997, 65.